Permission to Flourish

Breaking Free From Fear

Jai Cornell
Visionary Author

Copyright ©2024

All rights reserved.

Cover art, book design, and formatting by The Time Queen Co., Ltd.

No part of this book may be used or reproduced in any manner whatsoever without written permission by the author.

This book represents the collective effort of multiple co-authors, each sharing their personal viewpoints and experiences. It is a reflection of diverse perspectives, transcending differences in religion, spiritual beliefs, and viewpoints. Our intention is to bring together a mosaic of voices, fostering a sense of unity and expression without judgment. Please understand that the content within these pages is meant for exploration and understanding, and does not necessarily reflect any universal truths or consensus among the co-authors. We encourage readers to approach this book with an open heart and appreciation for the richness of human diversity.

All contributors to this work have duly consented to the use of their personal data, facts, recollections, memories, and / or experiences found herein. They are aware that the end and intended result was mass production and publication in connection with this work. As such, they have agreed without equivocation or caveat to indemnify, defend, and hold harmless the collaborator and publisher of this material, along with their affiliates, officers, directors, employees, and agents from any and all claims, damages, expenses, and liabilities arising out of or in connection with the use of such personal data, facts, recollections, memories, and experiences, including any claims of infringement of intellectual property rights or violation of privacy rights.

CONTENTS

INTRODUCTION
Permission to Flourish: Breaking Free From Fear
Jai Cornell..1

Chapter 1 **Transforming Grief into Resilience**..3
Niky Hamilton

Chapter 2 **Empowered by Choice: The Courage Within**..................................14
Beth Berghan

Chapter 3 **Navigating Fear and Courage: A Mother's Journey**........................25
Moon Sade

Chapter 4 **Reveal Your Inner Power: Finding Courage Amidst Adversity**..........36
Haig Mouradian

Chapter 5 **Heartbreak to Healing: A Journey of Unexpected Events and Self-Discovery**..................48
Di Challenor

Chapter 6 **Know Your Worth, Live Your Value**..........................58
  Elisa James

Chapter 7 **The Show Must Go On**..70
  Erin Coley

Chapter 8 **Fear Never Visits Just Once**......................................81
  Suellen Brook

Chapter 9 **Embracing Fear, Finding Inner Strength**................94
  Irene Gathuru

Chapter 10 **Embracing the Journey:**
  From Fear to Freedom..103
  Jaisha Rose

Chapter 11 **From "When" to "How"**..112
  Simonne Liley

Chapter 12 **Fearless**..124
  Jai Cornell

EPILOGUE

Jai Cornell..133

INTRODUCTION

PERMISSION TO FLOURISH: BREAKING FREE FROM FEAR

By Jai Cornell

Fear is regarded as a primal program that is instilled in every living creature. Fears can be innate, and fears can be learned through experience. It has long kept us safe from the world, preventing us from getting injured or killed by hazards or predators. But the rudimentary days of humanity have moved past the era of cavemen, early civilizations, and medieval threats.

We live in a time that is far more peaceful, advanced, and accepting than ever before, yet our brains have not evolved to match our new dilemmas. Fear continues to take the reins when it comes to protecting us, but the things it considers a threat are far from it. Fear wants us to believe that it's better to remain unchanged, stick to what we know, and never venture away from the path we've chosen. It doesn't matter if the path we are on could lead to pain, harm, or even death. The mind would rather know the outcome of the familiar instead of venturing into the unknown.

Permission to Flourish: Breaking from Fear is an anthology comprised of 12 chapters, each written by a coauthor, who has each come face-to-face with their own fears and has chosen a different path. They have faced the loss of loved ones, divorce, infidelity, verbal and physical abuse, financial struggles, homelessness, loss of self, career struggles, and so much more. Fear of loss, change, and the unknown once kept them from moving forward, but in their stories, you will see they found a way to leave fear behind. They used determination, conviction, and purpose in what they believed and learned to carve a new path forward.

As you read along with the stories on these pages, consider your own hardships with fear. What is it that you are afraid of right now? What is it that you are not doing because of fear? What would your life look like if fear were not there to hold you back?

In the end, remember that fear is something we must all face. It is possible to remain stuck, but it is also possible to find a way forward, too. Embrace the unknown, embrace change, and embrace the possibilities that lie ahead when you break free from fear.

Chapter 1

Transforming Grief into Resilience

Niky Hamilton

"There's no heartbeat."

I am staring back at the nurse in disbelief as she pushes and prods into my swollen belly with the foetal heart monitor. I glance over at my husband, who is leaning up against the hospital wall. I try to read the expression on his blank face. The wall clock beside him reads 07:40 p.m. We're supposed to be heading home soon for dinner.

Just one hour earlier, we had been taking a slow beach walk, listening to the steady rhythm of gentle waves on the shore. We watched the full moon rise over the ocean. Its reflection reached out towards our feet at the water's edge, stopping short of the wave break, not quite making it to shore.

I was two days overdue. As I took in the full moon's watery reflection, I voiced a concern that was forming in the depths of my heart. There had not been much baby movement that day.

It's probably nothing to worry about, but perhaps we should call the hospital and have a check-up? Just to be sure. We finished our walk, prepared dinner for our return, and drove to the hospital.

"I'm sorry, I can't find a heartbeat," the nurse says with a flustered look.

I watch her fumbling with the monitor, and I begin to wonder if she knows what she is doing. Perhaps she is a new graduate. Perhaps she's never used this equipment before. Has she even switched it on? Perhaps it's her first day on the maternity ward. Perhaps she's incompetent.

Another nurse strides in, and I feel a surge in confidence that this woman knows what she is doing. She'll sort it out, and then we can head home to dinner. She brings in a different monitor and rests it on my belly for the longest moment. Time slows along with my breath.

Silence fills the room.

Time starts to distort, and I watch the wall clock slide sideways like a Salvador Dali painting. I feel myself sinking, the room spins and everything blurs. There was a flurry of people, another nurse, an obstetrician I don't recognise, and an ultrasound scan.

Glenn, my husband, is now lying beside me, and I am having trouble breathing.

"There's no heartbeat. I'm sorry your baby has died. You'll stay here overnight and be induced to deliver him tomorrow," the staff says before taking their equipment and leaving Glenn and I in the now empty room.

Nothing is making sense. This can't be real. Is this real? This isn't real.

My body loses all feeling as it dissolves into the hospital bed. I sink below the surface and find myself underwater. I can't find air. I am trying to reach for the surface, but the water extends in all directions as far as the eye can see, out to infinity. I am lost. I can't breathe. I am drowning. The water's weight is crushing every cell in my body, and I feel like I am being torn into a million pieces.

The night lasts a lifetime as we lie awake, oscillating between numb disbelief and drowning despair.

Morning arrives, and with it brings the dawning realisation that I now need to give birth. I feel exhausted, numb, and beaten, but I have no time to rest. Before long, I find myself in the birthing suite with Glenn supporting me. The pain of induction hits me like a steam train, and I don't think I can bear this. I am begging for mercy, trying to crawl out of my body, and out of my life. Surely, I am dying?

Then, through the painful chaos, we enter the calm eye of a storm. Everything slows and turns silent. Without a sound, you, Baxter, were born with your perfect face, your perfect fingers, and your perfect tiny feet. Time slowed to a halt. Like a perfectly formed droplet of water paused at the end of a tap, we too were suspended here together, our breath held, in this perfect moment. I want this moment, suspended in time, to last forever. I place my hand on your heart and feel the enormity of this love.

But time loses its grip. The droplet releases and falls, crashing to the surface below. Time accelerates, and we are forced to let go, to leave you behind. I can barely feel my legs as I am carried down the hospital corridor towards the exit, sobbing in despair.

This is how I came to enter the world of grief. To find myself transformed from a happy, confident, ambitious woman, a physio, a presenter, and a high achieving business owner into an empty shell of my former self, unable to get dressed or string a sentence together.

The following week, after Baxter died, was a blur of friends and family. I recall standing with Glenn at his funeral, staring out at the sea of loving faces there to support us. I was struck with the image of a still lake holding a mountain's reflection. The depths of our sadness and our grief, were a reflection of the mountain of love that surrounded us. I felt a wave of gratitude that helped buoy us through those early days. I felt hope that maybe I would recover, bounce back somehow.

Then the early days turned into weeks, then into months, stretching out until I became aware that I would forever be missing a part of me. Bouncing back was just an illusion.

The daily exhaustion of grief meant my body felt like lead, and I could barely get out of bed. I struggled with memory loss, flashbacks, overwhelm, and brain fog—an emotional rollercoaster I had no control over. I lost confidence and trust in myself. I wandered the house aimlessly, feeling lost. Each day, I would find myself on the floor of Baxter's room, where his life lay suspended in time. I would see other women with children and feel overcome with resentment, jealousy, anger, and shame. I felt isolated and emotionally reactive.

I would spend hours ruminating on all the steps that led to that night. If only I'd changed one thing, kept my doctor appointments, chosen a different path, and made a different decision, then perhaps this would never have happened. With all of the what-ifs came a story of self-blame that added to the heavy chain of emotions I carried.

I was treading water in survival mode with a hole in my heart the size of the universe that no one else could see. I found myself feeling isolated, looking in at life from the outside, unable to participate. I knew I wanted to do more than just survive my life; I just didn't know how.

Months went by, and I knew I needed help. Help overcoming symptoms of trauma. Help overcoming grief, depression, and anxiety. Help finding direction through the emotional mess. Help overcoming the narrative of blame and resentment.

I tried counselling and psychologists. I dragged my body up a nearby mountain each day and went back to the gym. Surely, exercise would help, right? I tried yoga and meditation. I tried positive affirmations and mantras. If I just tried hard enough, would I go back to my normal positive self?

The harder I tried, the more elusive recovery appeared to be. Like walking up a steep sand dune, my heart would sink. Two steps forward, one step back—I forgot to pause and look at how far

I'd come rather than how far I had to go. In the midst of all the trying, I grieved what we had lost. I grieved the future I thought we'd have. I grieved the loss of myself—the person I used to be, the person that no longer existed. I was exhausted trying to form a new picture from the rubble that surrounded me.

I lived here in the depths for a long time, without solutions, without direction. Telling the same story to different counsellors in a circular, dusty path.

Then one day, a close friend approached me and offered to take me on her yoga retreat in Bali for a week. She knew I had been struggling and was offering this generous gift as a chance to take time out.

My initial response was to say, "No, I can't possibly do that! That would mean leaving the house, facing other women, and leaving Baxter's room!"

I reflected and realised I was saying 'no' for two different reasons.

The first was I'd spent my whole life prioritising everyone else's needs. I had no idea how to prioritise my own without a sense of guilt. Saying 'yes' to receiving felt foreign.

The next reason was my sense of worthiness. With everything that had happened, with all of the what-ifs and the story of self-blame, came the belief that I don't deserve this. I don't deserve joy, love, or anything positive for myself.

By chance, at that moment, I came across a Dr. Demartini quote that read, "Whatever you have or have not done, you are worthy of love."

Something deep inside me stirred. Despite everything, I am still worthy of love.

I knew something had to change. My health was suffering, my work was suffering, and my mental health was suffering.

I knew I had reached a crossroads and needed to make a choice. I could keep walking this familiar path of self-blame, resentment, and despair. This path that felt like it kept me connected to our son, looking backwards at the life we'd lost.

Or I could take one step onto a new and unknown path. One that started with prioritising me and believing that I was worthy. I hesitated, afraid it meant I would start moving on. Yet, I knew something had to change.

This was my first lesson through grief: I was worthy and needed to start prioritising me.

I came to realise I had spent months dreaming of the life I thought I'd have by comparing my life to the women around me, comparing my life to what I thought it should be, and ruminating on what we had lost.

The next lesson I learned through grief was to let go of comparisons with others and what life should be. In the space of letting go, the resentment, the sadness, and the injustice of it all started to lift like a fog. In the presence of what is, I discovered a stillness in my broken heart that became an open, guiding light to steer me through the rubble.

Saying 'yes' to that retreat was my first step towards resilience. I reflected on what I needed and had time to search my heart for direction. I became clear on my inner strengths, what was important to me, and my values. I made the decision to learn how to navigate my emotional rollercoaster, how to steer my self-talk, and how to trust my heart. From there, I created a step-by-step pathway to guide me—*moving with* rather than *moving on.* It's these steps that I now share to help women rise up and find direction through grief.

Grief can take many faces and forms: death, loss, relationship breakdown, family separation, health problems, career setbacks, or a life we thought we'd have. We find ourselves staring at rubble and wondering where to start.

My final lesson through grief was to understand and honour my values and use my strengths to pull me through. With this lesson, I've found both direction and heart-centred authenticity.

The family I thought we'd have was never realised. As I gaze out to the women I have helped through grief, like a mirrored lake's reflection, I feel the family I have created is simply in a different form. With gratitude, I know that love is grief's reflection.

We all have a choice: to stay circling in the story of sadness, resentment, and blame, dreaming of the life we thought we'd have; or to step out into the unknown with the knowledge that we are worthy, to let go of comparisons, to allow our broken hearts to open and light the way forward, and to dig deep to find our unique strengths and values to find clarity and authentic direction.

"Resilience is not about bouncing back.
It's about our heart's courageous choice to transform."
-Niky Hamilton

About the Author
Niky Hamilton

Niky Hamilton is a grief expert and speaker, women's resilience coach, physiotherapist, a heart-centered leader, and business owner. Her qualifications also include NLP Master Coach and Dr. Demartini Facilitator.

Niky's mission is to help women build resilience and find direction through grief and life's losses. Her work helps women who feel depleted or overwhelmed through life's losses to find courage, clarity, and confidence. She regularly hosts her Rise UP resilience retreats, as well as offering her coaching program.

She combines her expertise as a qualified health practitioner and coach with her heartfelt personal experience to guide women through the rubble. Her unique approach helps women build resilience through the messiness of life by rebuilding from the ground up.

Contact Information

Email: niky@synergywomen.com.au
Website: www.nikyhamilton.com

Chapter 2

Empowered by Choice: The Courage Within

Beth Berghan

What should I do? What can I do? What does the future hold?

Should I stay in my marriage and deal with the toxic behaviour and affairs, or should I draw on my certainty, confidence, and courage to end it? Should I keep my sons (aged 3 and 1) in a family home with both parents, or should I remove one parent from the family picture and deal with the potential emotional fallout? Should I choose to stay in this new house, or could I find somewhere else to create a home?

Looking back, there were so many signs. Things that seemed insignificant individually became one huge red flag the day I discovered a mobile phone account, which clearly showed that he was still having an affair. Calls at all times of the day and night. Calls at times when he was with us, his family, or friends. Calls, which told me he was not actively engaged with his kids or fully committed to making our marriage work. His response? Change the billing address so I no longer had access to it.

My youngest son was always a little tentative around his father, and this was becoming more obvious. My eldest son was losing his sense of independence, becoming unsettled and clingy when I left him to go to work. Late nights and very early mornings meant they were both seeing much less of their father, who was prioritising his affair over work and home.

I began noticing the consistent attempts to put me down. This hadn't been a thing in the earlier years of our relationship, so it was out of character— or so I thought. My response to his consistent and rude comments about my body set a pattern that served me immediately and right through the challenging times that followed.

I chose to take my power back by controlling what I could control. I did this by always getting changed in the bathroom with the door closed and by wearing an old loose t-shirt and undies to bed—one of the rare times in my life I didn't sleep naked. And, to my joy, what I discovered was that my deliberate choice to do this made me feel powerful, confident, and strong. I was actively and calmly rejecting his behaviour without getting into an emotional yelling match, fueled by asking him to stop putting me down.

I took control of the situation and showed up strong for myself. Most importantly, I showed him my strength as well, weakening him in the process. I showed him that I believed in myself and that my actions would speak for me and support my beliefs and values. I chose me.

And every time I took my clothes into the ensuite and closed the door behind me, I told myself these things:
"I am worthy."
"I don't need his approval. I have my own."
"I am self-sufficient."
"I place high value on myself."
"I love myself way too much to settle."

The payoff from taking this approach was that I didn't get angry about his behaviour or let other negative emotions wash over me because I was positively reinforcing my self-belief. I was choosing my response to his behaviour, empowering myself through choice.

There it is again. The power of CHOICE. I found that choice combined with courage, strength, discipline, focus, and a commitment to have fun meant that it was easy to maintain a positive mindset. Day in and day out, living my values and raising my sons in a positive and loving family environment became normal. I won't lie; some days, this was a whole heap easier than others.

I remember times of deep reflection when I was asking myself, "What are the lessons here? What am I learning about myself, him (ex-husband), my kids, and the situation? Where do I need to make changes to prevent myself from getting overwhelmed as a single parent?"

For more than 9 months, I had ridden a roller coaster. Up into the dizzying heights of realising that he was not going to change, that our values were not aligned, and that I had the strength and self-belief to deal with being a single parent. Down, down, down into the darker depths of wondering how I could possibly move my sons away from living with their father, wondering how they would cope and how I might cope on my own. Up, up, up high to the financial certainty of a secure, full-time job. Down, down, down to wondering how I would manage financially and succeed at parenting with no immediate family support within 1,600 kilometres and most of them in another country. Up, up, up to being certain that this was the example I wanted to set for my children. Down, down, down to wondering if there was more I could have done to maintain and save the marriage.

All this internal processing was playing havoc with my gut, tight as a drum, and filled with many different emotions. My gut felt so tight that I barely ate anything most days, as I had no appetite. The good thing was that this tightness absorbed the bulk of the emotions, pressure, and stress, which left my mindset clear and positively focused on looking after my sons, looking after myself as best as I could, and being professional and productive at my job. Just to keep me on my toes, I was in the final 12 months of a psychology degree as an external student at the same time.

The more I reflected, the more lessons became obvious to me, and these consolidated over time. I learned that it would take courage to follow my heart, and that I had courage to spare. I learned to trust myself, my instincts, and my capability. I learned to focus forward to the next step, and the one after that, rather than looking backwards, stuck in negative emotions. I learned to dig deep into my untapped strength because I had whatever strength it would take.

Most importantly, I learned that no one can ever remove my ability to choose—to choose what happens next, my attitude, what I say, and what I do. The choice ALWAYS remains with me.

It's kind of like when it's time to replace your favourite pair of jeans. You put them on, and they feel great. They fit, they are soft, and they hug you like an old friend. You feel comfortable in them and love styling them. Your friends all wear them too, so you feel accepted and part of the tribe. You are keen for more skinny jeans.

But when you check out the stores, the fashion has changed.

Skinny jeans are out. Totally, no longer a thing. High-waisted, wide-leg jeans are having their moment. They are all the rage.

Right here, just as in my situation, things get tough, and a decision needs to be made. Do you stick with the comfort of what you know, like, and enjoy wearing, or do you step out of your comfort zone and go try on a new pair of wide-leg jeans?

Do you stick with the relationship because, even though it's not working for you and your children, it represents security and comfort? Or do you trust yourself enough to embrace the unknown and potential growth and adventure that leaving will bring?

Imagine for a moment that you were in this very same situation. What would you do if you were here? How would you decide?

Would you stay and put up with it, knowing that the best indicator of future behaviour is past behaviour and that he was not likely to change? Would you choose this kind of security over being gaslit and losing your own self-worth, or would you take a couple of deep breaths and step out into the unknown?

I chose the wide-leg jeans, the unknown, the potential growth, and the adventure.

It had been a day like any other. I struggled to get my sons to sleep, and their father got home very late. However, the following morning was different. I bolted upright in bed. My bedside clock glowed at 3:48 a.m. Quite suddenly, not only was I fully awake physically, but I was also emotionally and mentally aware with great clarity and focus. I felt a door opening somewhere in me. A new door, which led to a happy home for me and my boys. A home where love, positivity, and laughter prevailed—where FUN was mandatory.

My focus was forward, confirming that there was no need to stay stuck and that I had done enough now to try to save the marriage. My energy would be better spent being the best parent and person I could be as a role model for my sons.

Simultaneously, I felt a surge of certainty and self-belief saying, "I've got this!" I took several deep breaths to fill my head and my heart with a commitment to trust myself, to enjoy myself, and to live a life that mattered through continuous personal growth.

In that moment of clarity, the decision was made, and my marriage was over. I hugged myself and started planning the next 24 hours.

Yep!! The next 24 hours, those were the ones that really mattered. I needed to figure out how to show up for myself and for my sons and figure out who I needed to talk to and what to tell them. Hour by hour, step by step, building certainty and courage would help me take that first step into the unknown, the first day to the rest of my new life.

When I look back on this period of my life, I realise that it was the only time as an adult that I wrote a daily diary. This was very different from the journaling I do now to reflect on my thoughts and feelings, as it was more of an opportunity for me to voice what I was going through. It was a powerful confidant, meeting me where I was at every single day without judgement. I needed that, and you might too.

Uprooting your life and the lives of your kids by ending a marriage is never going to be an easy decision. Like me, you may toy with the final decision over time until you are certain about your choice. You may leave and come back. You may need to build your strength and certainty.

I ended my marriage, confident that this was the absolute end and that there was no coming back, no reconciliation. I knew I would be able to look my sons in the eye and tell them, "I did everything I could, and I gave it my all. I stayed longer than many other women would have."

This certainty came from knowing that I was not getting what I needed, wanted, and deserved in my marriage. I would encourage you to ask yourself if you are getting what you need, want, and deserve, and to set clear boundaries of what you will accept in any situation.

A failing marriage or relationship is always going to be an emotional time, especially if there are children involved. Find those trusted friends you can be raw and vulnerable with, and actively seek their perspective and guidance. It's okay to cry, rant, howl, and sleep – you will need it.

Remind yourself that every single ending is actually a new beginning. Lean into and embrace the adventure.

Remind yourself that this new adventure is only going to be as hard as you choose to make it.

And remind yourself that "Do I want to be in this situation?" is the first question you must answer before you move on to, "What will I do now?"

Choose to tap into your courage, and a whole new life will unfold for you. Remember, there is always a choice, and the choice is always yours.

About the Author
Beth Berghan

Beth Berghan provides confidential coaching for executives and business owners, working with individuals and teams in building exceptional leadership, communication, and mental fitness skills. She regularly facilitates group workshops, influencing transformation in team communication and behaviours.

Beth has an extensive coaching toolkit including Positive Intelligence, Happiness Coach, NLP Master Coach & Time Line Therapy. Her coaching focus is self-leadership – leadership and communication from the inside out. Beth insists on celebrating every single achievement with her clients to anchor in successful behaviours and breed further success.

Beth, an internationally awarded coach, is an impactful speaker and MC who loves sharing her knowledge, both live and online, with the goal of influencing change and breakthroughs for her audience. She is authentic, warm, confident, and creative, has a strong sense of fun and a passionate commitment to having every single person recognize the potency of their greatest superpower— the power of choice.

Contact Information

WhatsApp:

+617412585148

Website:

www.bethberghan.com

Email:

coach@bethberghan.com

LinkedIn:

www.linkedin.com.au/in/bethberghan

Facebook:

www.facebook.com/bethberghan

Instagram:

www.instagram.com/bethberghan

30-Min Chat :

https://calendly.com/bethberghancoach/30-minute

Chapter 3

Navigating Fear and Courage: A Mother's Journey

Moon Sade

"In the journey of a lifetime, one step forward every day is all it takes."
-Moon Sade

Looking back now, I can clearly see two faces—fear and courage—and how they shaped my choices in life, for worse and for better. One of those faces might be shaping your choices right now. The question is, which one?

My story unfolds in two places at once, driven in different ways in both instances by my bright and uniquely individual autistic children. Eventually, it built to a point where the "sweet little" face of the fear that had driven me for years finally unmasked itself and was revealed as the architect of the ever-narrowing gap in the 'rock and the hard place' that I had existed in for, what seemed like, forever.

I watched my children—the eldest, already changed by years of dismissal and being misunderstood; and the younger, so innocent and sweet, but fated to walk the same path as his older brother, unless I stepped around the blind bend of the turning point in front of me and changed things.

Knowing the time was NOW, my heart was pounding like never before. I felt every quiver in my being as I looked into the raging face of the gaping fear in front of me, filled with uncertainty at the choice I was about to make.

To understand the path I'm on, you have to know the beginning, where it all started more than 20 years ago with my eldest child.

When my oldest was little, we noticed differences in the way he did things: how he played with and without toys, interacted with people, reacted to things, and responded to what was happening around him. Small, slight differences, not so significant that they could be easily noticed or picked up on, but the type of signs parents notice, bringing with it the natural parental fear of what the future would hold for him, and the desire to take steps to ensure these differences didn't stand in his way.

These early signs of developmental differences didn't fit the stereotypically expected ones of autism. He was a bright, intelligent child who, very early on, became a master at masking and mimicking.

Our concerns were dismissed, ignored, and overlooked by those eager to see only what they wanted. And I? I was too afraid of the repercussions on my child, too worried about upsetting the apple cart, too concerned about my job and the plans I had, and too afraid to raise my voice and demand something be done.

So, what I didn't want to have happen, began to happen …

I could see my child starting to slip through the cracks of a system that didn't understand him or the help he needed. They saw him only as a disruptive, undisciplined, unfocused child—deserving of less attention and not needing more.

Determined not to let that happen, without upsetting the apple cart, I used the resources and skills at my disposal as a qualified, full-time high school teacher. We started putting strategies and techniques in place at home to help him. I knew he needed more. Every day we tried different things, sometimes learning painfully, through trial and error, what worked for him specifically and what didn't. We continued adding new strategies and techniques, and including special tools to be used at home. But only at home, because no matter how many years went by, no matter how many helpless meetings we held with his educational providers, highlighting the differences so clearly evident to us, each and every time, our concerns were dismissed.

So, we struggled on our own. It became a constant balancing act for us and our once happy, smiling, laughing child.

Time went on, years passed, and in the way of families like ours, while we were happy, we also became more isolated, more lonely, more marginalised, and more inwardly focused. We struggled with working things out on our own, doing things by ourselves, and being continuously ignored or misunderstood.

We were dismissed when our concerns were raised. Days, weeks, months, and years were spent searching, often not finding the answers we were looking for. We were lost in the generalised, sometimes inaccurate information out there, feeling more and more alone. All the while, I was frantically juggling to successfully maintain my full-time, highly demanding, highly stressful teaching job. I didn't know I was walking my way towards the perfect storm that was brewing ahead of me.

That perfect storm came with the birth of my second child.

The years of juggling, struggling, balancing, and making futile efforts to change things for my child in a meaningful way came to a head when stress and teacher burnout met postnatal depression head-on.

That's when everything changed! I was forced to stop and look around, to really SEE my world. Suddenly, everything looked different. I was looking at the world from a whole new perspective, and I didn't like what I was seeing.

As I watched my child cradle his baby brother on his lap, I was struck by the realisation that while I had been doing my best for my other 'kids' —my students—I had been mistakenly expecting others to do their best for my child, which they weren't.

With that realisation came a moment of clarity. If I wanted someone to do their best for my boys, it was going to have to be me, and I couldn't do it on a part-time basis.

Deep down inside, I knew what that meant, but I fought against it. I had all the reasons why nothing should change and constantly argued with myself. Surely, I didn't have to be that dramatic? prospects for progression and better pay. That would benefit my children, wouldn't it? Imagine all the things I could put in place for them with that money—the help I could afford to pay for. Besides, doing without my salary would have a massive impact on us as a family. How could that be good for us?

No matter what arguments I put forward, one truth remained: if I wanted something different for my children, I was going to have to make a different choice.

Knowing the time was now, my hands shaking, filled with uncertainty at what the future would bring, what my decision would mean for us, feeling the fear in every fibre of my being but still determined to do it, I typed up my resignation letter and emailed it to the HR department. I wouldn't be returning after maternity leave. It was done, and my life has never been the same.

In the years that followed, we faced emotional, mental, physical, and financial hardships and difficulties. We've known what it is to be homeless and hungry, but by the grace of God, we've moved past it. Life continues to have its share of challenges. It would be unrealistic to expect otherwise. In general, it is the nature of life, and definitely the nature of living with and parenting autistics.

Even so, that decision to prioritise my family shifted the course of everything. It was as though a veil had parted, and I had clear sight. It has made a world of difference to me, my children, my family, the steps I took moving forward, the passion I found within myself, my vision for the future, my roles in life, and the business I'm building today—helping young, autistic adults.

With the newfound time I had and armed with my years as a teacher, who worked with a wide and varied range of students, I could now build up a list of the differences I noticed in my child with the tools, techniques, and strategies we had at home compared to the absence of them at school. Finally, after almost a decade of asking and being ignored, I had the evidence I needed for my eldest child to start a formal assessment of his developmental and educational differences.

The assessment process took time, but eventually, just before he turned 17, my oldest was formally diagnosed with high-functioning autism. It was only possible because I was now present every day, making sure he didn't fall through the cracks again! Now, I was able to ask for and be given the allowances, help, and accom-modations he needed. He could finally have the same tools and strategies in an educational setting, which complemented those he had at home, to give him the opportunity to rise above other people's misconceptions and the flawed expectations that had followed him since the age of 4.

Having that formal diagnosis for my eldest child meant that when I raised my concern about my younger child, I was listened to. That, and being able to offer evidence and examples from all the time spent with him—the result of walking away from my teaching career to focus on my family.

The road to assessment and diagnosis for my younger child was so completely different. The choice was made early on to take his education a different route so he could develop naturally, without the stigma and pressure to conform like his brother had to endure. My presence, my observations and awareness, my growing willingness and ability to advocate clearly and confidently for my child, my older child's struggles and his diagnosis—all combined to speed up the process for my younger child. By the time he was 5 years old, he was assessed as having ASD+. All of this has and continues to shape so much of his acceptance of his world, his life, his approach to himself, and his autism.

In the years since I felt 'that' fear and stepped forward anyway, my children aren't the only ones who have had the benefit of time and attention. There are times I hardly recognise myself as the person I was.

I spent the first few years just focusing on my children and making sure I was doing whatever I had to to put in place the things they needed. In doing that, I began to truly learn about myself, which began my ongoing journey of personal development and growth.

Over time, I realised my own neurodivergence. I recognised my resilience, drive, determination, strengths, skills, abilities, and desire to make a difference. Through coaching and mentoring, I found a different way to combine my knowledge and experience, which is to teach and educate.

But something was missing.

Knowing how isolating the years had been for us, how lonely and confusing at times, and how many families, teenagers, and young autistic adults silently struggle every day, I had to make another choice. I could stay safely in the shadows and keep doing what I was doing, or I could continue on the path I'd chosen all those years ago. I could step forward, despite my fear, and share my story as a neurodivergent woman parenting autistic children. More than that, I could use my skills, knowledge, and experience to guide the future of so many young autistic adults by helping them step out of the misconceptions and flawed expectations of others.

Recognising this as another turning point, I reflected on the changes of the last few years. I finally realised the power of choosing courage over fear as I deliberated on whether I wanted to go back to letting my fears drive me or to hold my head high and move forward on my own terms every day.

That's exactly what I do! I'm proud to say that—I'm Moon Sade, and I'm an Autism Success Mentor, choosing courage over fear and taking one step forward every day.

About the Author
Moon Sade

Moon Sade is an Autism Success Mentor, who is passionate about empowering young autistic adults. She centres her work on guiding autistic youth, ages 17-25, through the complexities of their journey into adulthood. Her framework uniquely integrates 25+ years of personal experience with certifications in Understanding Autism, Life Coaching, NLP, and Time Line Therapy.

Her experience as a high school teacher grants her profound insight into the specific challenges her mentees face, uniquely equipping her to guide them through their journey with a customised approach. She offers personalised mentoring tailored to each mentee's distinct aspirations and challenges. Grounded in adaptability, compassion, and an unwavering commitment to fostering fundamental change, her approach transcends mere mentorship. With her, individuals uncover more than a mentor; they discover a guide who comprehends the intricacies of their journey and empowers them to thrive independently.

Contact Information

Phone Number:

+44 7863 715 489

Email:

hello@autism-in-disguise.com

Facebook:

https://www.facebook.com/moon.sade.754

Website:

www.autism-in-disguise.com

Chapter 4

Reveal Your Inner Power: Finding Courage Amidst Adversity

Haig Mouradian

What if, in the next 5 years, you stayed in the exact same position you're in right now? How would that look like, knowing that nothing has changed for you? This was the question that turned my whole life around.

Back in 2019, when I was on the verge of depression. I was disgusted by life, people, and my poor choices and decisions. I was letting myself down in every possible way. Lost, confused, and stuck in a messed up reality, I found myself wishing, hoping, pleading, and begging for things to be different. Yet, I didn't even know what I wanted to do with my life at that point. I was living in mediocrity. I weighed 106 kilograms (234 pounds), smoked two packs of cigarettes a day, was in and out of relationships, and hated my job. I was mentally out of shape, lacking self-love, confidence, and trust in myself. My life was a total mess, and I was consistently stuck in a cycle of self-doubt and negativity, trapped in a prison I couldn't escape. I resorted to binge eating almost every day to numb myself, hoping to wake up to a different life.

Let's go back in time to see how I actually got to this point in my life. Back in my school days, I constantly compared myself to others, feeling shame for needing private tutors to keep up. Despite my efforts, my grades never quite measured up, reinforcing my belief that I was just an average individual destined for mediocrity. This perception followed me into university, where a single criticism from an economics teacher about my English proficiency struck me to my core. The humiliation and fear of judgment consumed me, paralyzing me with the thought that I was fundamentally inadequate.

As I transitioned into adulthood, the echoes of my school days continued to reverberate, amplifying my insecurities in ways that I never imagined. I vividly recall several incidents in my career when I received comments about needing a "confident and smart" person in the team to handle important and high-quality tasks. This only deepened my insecurities, convincing me that I would never be enough.

Among many other things that went on, all these experiences contributed to a cycle of self-loathing and insecurity that plagued me throughout my life. They became the soundtrack to my self-doubt, drowning out any semblance of confidence or self-assurance. I internalized labels like: " I'm not smart enough, not qualified enough, who am I kidding? I'm just average, no one would listen to me or appreciate what I do." I didn't realize the impact they had on my mindset and behaviour. Little did I know, the subconscious doesn't distinguish between constructive and destructive, and I unknowingly projected this energy into the world.

I became hyper-aware of what others thought of me, allowing their opinions to dictate my every move. Even when I was confident in my choices or had glimpses of my potential and was praised for my work, I still second-guessed myself and put others' approval before my own. I found it really hard to accept compliments or acknowledge my strengths. I couldn't believe or trust myself. This made me hold on to my insecurities tightly, which controlled and dictated my thoughts and actions every day. And every time I missed an opportunity to challenge those limiting beliefs, it only made things even worse. It was a frustrating cycle that I carried with me for far too long and that caused me to feel unworthy.

However, amidst this wild journey, there came a turning point that changed everything. It was when I stumbled upon an advertisement featuring Tony Robbins and Dean Graziosi. Dean asked the question, "What if, in the next 5 years, you stayed in the exact same position you're in right now?"

That question forced me to confront the reality of my situation, igniting a fire within me to make a change. I couldn't bear the thought of wasting another five years of my life. I knew I needed to take action, step out of my comfort zone, and create the life I always desired. It was the first time I actually listened to that inner voice, trusted myself, and approached things without seeking external validation.

Leaving behind my job, my relationship, and my country, I embarked on a journey of self-discovery to Rome. Rome became my sanctuary, where I sought clarity, purpose, and meaning in my life. Throughout that period, I fully and deeply immersed myself in personal development and invested in multiple online courses, workshops, and programs to better myself. I was so blessed and grateful that I found the space and solitude to wholeheartedly delve into this transformative process. It truly was a period of intense growth and self-discovery.

During my time of healing, I had a profound realization: I was the cause of everything happening in my life. Although it was a very hard pill to swallow at first, eventually, with time, I figured that if I truly wanted to change my life, I had to take responsibility for my decisions, beliefs, and actions. That's when I started to consciously and purposefully do the inner work day in and day out, confronting my fears and limiting beliefs head-on.

Within a year, I underwent a remarkable transformation. I lost 14 kilograms of weight (almost 31 pounds), quit smoking, and embraced personal growth wholeheartedly. I let go of anything that no longer served me and shifted my focus toward abundance and success.

I will never forget the moment I returned to my home country, Jordan, transformed into a new person. I was a new, confident, and unstoppable being who wasn't settling for less and who was fully committed to creating and tapping into the life I truly wanted. If my past self had met this new version of me, he definitely would've been a stranger to him.

I remember stepping into my room for the first time after a long year. It truly was nostalgic. I started recalling memories of the person I used to be, and in that moment, I remember closing my eyes, allowing myself to drift back in time, and actually visualized my past self lying on the bed under a thick blanket, feeling depressed, hopeless, and exhausted. I approached him, held his hands gently, looked him in the eyes, and whispered, "Life will never be the same again, buddy. You've got this!"

To this day, it still gives me chills. Truly, since then, life has never been the same again.

Fast forward to now, I've embarked on a quest to help others. As a transformational life coach, I support young, ambitious, and passionate millennials get unstuck from their current reality, break free from their limitations, and discover the greatness, brilliance, and magnificence of who they truly are. My mission is to help them take control of their lives, live life on their own terms, and create purposeful and enriching journeys for themselves.

So, I share my story, not to impress you but to impress upon you that transformation is possible. If I can do it, I reckon you can do it too!!

Because of what I went through, I honestly thought I would be trapped in the "comfort zone" prison for a long time. I later realized that there was actually a way out. I found out, if I knew back then what I know now, I definitely would've been able to change my life's direction, be unstoppable, and save myself years and years of pain and suffering. But it's because of that pain and suffering that I am the me that I am now, and I wouldn't change that.

And so, I would love to end this chapter by sharing 5 incredible and hard-hitting lessons using the "POWER" acronym that has helped me tremendously throughout my journey. I'm hoping it will support, inspire, influence, and empower you in your journey as well.

P.O.W.E.R

Potential: You have the ultimate potential to live an extraordinary, outstanding, and incredible life, but only if you choose to. Change is a choice, growth is a choice, and playing small is also a choice.

Don't you dare wait until the discomfort and pain of staying the same becomes more unbearable than embracing change. Make a conscious and deliberate decision today to start changing your life and create the life you've always desired.

Always remember, life happens by choice, not by chance. You have the absolute power to choose how you want to live your life.

Opportunities: Focus your time, effort, and attention on the opportunities that are coming your way, not on your obstacles.

Learn from all the challenges, obstacles, and difficulties that life is throwing at you as they're put there for a reason—to learn and grow. However, give more emphasis and weight to your opportunities, because whatever you put your focus and energy into, it grows and expands, and eventually you will attract more of that in your life.

Always notice and be intentional with whatever you're focusing on.

Where you are right now and where you want to go: It's of the utmost importance to know and understand very clearly where you currently are in your life right now and where you're headed.

I want you to contemplate and ask yourself:
-How am I showing up in my health, career, relationships, and all other areas of my life?

Once you're clear about that, let your mind ponder around these questions:
-Where do I want to be?
-What do I want to have happen in the next 5 -10 years of my life?
-What's the most exciting and grandest vision I have for my life?

And even if you don't know and you're clueless about what the answer(s) are for you, just make it up, create it, and have fun doing so.

Enter - What are you allowing to enter your mind?: You are what you consistently feed your mind with. You're the books you read, the movies you watch, the music you listen to, the conversation you engage in, and the people you spend time with.

It's very important to stand guard at the gate of your mind and be aware of what you're stuffing it with because the seeds you plant are what will grow. If you don't intentionally feed your mind with success, it will rot with mediocrity.

Start consciously and deliberately feeding your mind with thoughts of abundance, success, prosperity, health, and happiness!

Remember, transformation always begins within the mind first before blossoming, revealing, and manifesting outwardly into the world.

Revealing your inner hero: We all have this incredible and powerful inner hero in each and every single one of us who is waiting to be fired up and unleashed to the world.

So don't you dare stay trapped in your comfort zone, dim your light, and deprive the world of your unique gifts, because it's not going to get you anywhere.

Get out of that prison and start stepping into your growth zone. Own, claim, and celebrate your magnificence because your family needs you, your community needs you, and the whole world needs you to step into that best version of yourself.

Always remember, to get things you never had, you've got to do things you never did. You must start showing up, even when it's scary, uncomfortable, and risky, because that's where your next level lives.

Step into what you're most hesitant about and have the courage to continue facing it head-on. Your power will emerge from there, guiding you towards your greatest potential.

> *"To create that next phenomenal, remarkable, and outstanding chapter of your life, you must be brave enough to close the current chapter you're rooted in."*
> -Haig Mouradian

Keep letting go of what isn't serving you anymore: old stories, attachments, promises, and heavy emotional baggage you've been holding onto for a long time. It's time for you to dump and flush them out of your system as they're not welcomed, invited, or meant to come with you in this incredible next chapter. Start making space and room for what's meant for you. Start saying 'yes' to your higher self, 'yes' to your mission, and 'yes' to your vision.

Start taking responsibility for the good, bad, and ugly. Start sacrificing for what you want so that you get to live and lead a life of choice, possibility, and freedom.

Unapologetically step into that newly courageous, bold, and badass YOU because your future self is counting on it!!

Absolutely crush it, super legend!! You've got this!!!

About the Author
Haig Mouradian

Haig Mouradian is a passionate, soul-driven transformational coach hailing from the heart of Jordan.
He inspires and guides young, ambitious souls to break free from limitations, discover their brilliance, and take charge of their destiny. Certified by Joel Brown's Influential Coaching and a distinguished member of the Global Coaches Association, Haig's expertise in NLP and Time Line Therapy enriches his transformative journey. He is currently leading the 5-Day Overwhelm to Clarity Challenge, inviting souls to embark on a journey of self-discovery and empowerment. Haig's mission is to ignite a world of brilliance through authentic connection and self-expression.

> *"To create that next phenomenal, remarkable, and outstanding chapter of your life, you must be brave enough to close the current one you're rooted in."*
> *-Haig Mouradian*

Contact information :

Facebook: Haig Mouradian
Instagram: @Iamhaigmouradian

Chapter 5

Heartbreak to Healing: A Journey of Unexpected Events and Self-Discovery

Di Challenor

Have you ever been to a haunted house? Do you recall that chilling fear that looms over you—the terror that you never know what might pop out at any moment? You know that someone or something is going to jump out of the dark. You know what to expect, and yet, you're still surprised when it happens because the timing of it all is unexpected.

That's exactly how life is.

Expected events at unexpected times made up most of the major milestones that happened in my life. I felt uncertainty, abandonment, fear, confusion, loneliness, and betrayal, and I wondered, "Why me?"

These events, back then, shaped me into a person I was not proud to be. Maybe you can relate?

Are you someone who feels abandoned or alone? Are you someone who focuses on your career or builds a business with no time for a romantic relationship? Do you enjoy your own company because you find it safer to be alone rather than to be let down, disappointed, used, or ignored by people who claim they care? Do you have weak boundaries and tend to be a people pleaser to keep everyone else happy? Do you prioritize others over yourself because that's what you were taught growing up? Are you attracted to unavailable or narcissistic partners? Or are you in or have been in codependent relationships because you always put others first? Do you think it must be them that needs help? Or that you have the ability to fix your broken marriage or relationship?

Have you answered "yes" to any of these questions?

Welcome to the club! This is who I was, but that's not who I am anymore. I became aware that I was doing everything I could to keep myself safe from having a broken heart by doing everything I thought was expected of me. Of course, the expected is never always certain.

Let's go back, back to what I consider the most unexpected but expected event that ever happened in my life…

It was the school holidays. We were staying at our beach house.

Imagine six kids and two adults. The main house wasn't big enough for all of us, so two kids slept in the caravan that came with the house. On this particular night, for some reason, I was sleeping on a banana lounge in the family room.

The next morning, my stepmother called out to me, "Come quick! It's your father!"

I found out just how hard it was to get out of a banana lounge when you're in a hurry! Wrestling myself free, I stumbled over to where she was. She was in the main bedroom, doing mouth-to-mouth on my dad.

"He doesn't look very good! He's blue!" I frantically said.

She told me to call an ambulance, but the beach house did not have a phone. A few of us had to walk the streets in our pyjamas to knock on doors and find a phone. Mobile phones were only a 'space-age' idea back then.

When the ambulance arrived, he was transported to the hospital, but it was too late. He had already passed away at the beach house, and we didn't get the chance to go to the hospital. His death was sudden and unexpected, so an autopsy was done. I was shattered about his passing! I didn't get to say good bye!

My stepmother told us what happened, that dad was getting up for the day and went into some sort of fit, and that was it. He had a sudden heart attack. According to my beliefs, based on the teachings of Louise L Hay, a heart attack represents a broken heart. In essence, my dad died from his heart being broken when my mum, his wife of 20 years and the love of his life, died only 3 years earlier from illness.

The autopsy for my dad revealed that his heart was tight as a result of holding in emotions. Yes, that was him. He didn't open up much from what I remember. I made a decision to become more open emotionally, to wear my heart on my sleeve. I believe it's okay to show and share emotions and be vulnerable with people you can trust. I haven't always picked the 'right' people to trust because my discernment has been missing in action for years! The good news is that my discernment is back and stronger than ever!

For a moment, I believed my parents passing was a journey I needed to confront, but I realised it was not a path meant for me. Their passing was their journey to follow, and my journey was taking me down another path. A path that was influenced by their passing, but not directly.

I decided to return to university to complete a degree in psychology, which helped me to align with my spiritual work, to experience the counselling process, and to find quick and easy healing tools to navigate the root cause of an emotional issue quickly, release it, heal it, and move on.

I was also on my own journey of self-healing, working with healers and fine tuning my healing skills. I learned that the subconscious mind stores everything for our soul's journey. When you are consciously ready, old wounds and pain will surface to be healed and easily dispersed. I recommend you do the inner work and deal with your emotional issues. If you need help, hire a practitioner who will resonate with you. You never know what will be uncovered by someone who is heart-centered and fully committed to helping and healing you.

After my first year of university, just a year after my dad's passing, my stepmother told me that I needed to leave the family home and grow up. I have to admit, I did not see this coming. One day, I knew I needed to leave, but not now. I had nowhere to go, and my friends were all still living at home. The feeling of loneliness and abandonment consumed me, but in a way, this was the Universe teaching me another lesson. The lesson I learned was that I would never allow someone to remove me from my home again. I was determined to find somewhere to be mine, all mine. However, until I could make that happen, the Universe put me on a different path.

It was my grandparents who took me in after this and let me stay upstairs in their attic. At first, it was strange living with much older people who had their own routines, but I felt loved and supported. They were genuinely interested in what I was learning and doing. Living with them was exactly what I needed to heal in the year that we lived together. At the end of the year, my brother was in the same situation I was in – homeless and nowhere to go. We decided to get a flat together, and we had fun for two years.

A few years later, my stepmother gave my siblings and I our former family home back. Being in the house again stirred up a lot of old family memories. I recall that this was the first time I saw a wavering light, like a ghost. It wasn't scary. I believe that it was my mum showing herself to me. My mum had passed in this house, but not in the room that I saw the light. In fact, I had even predicted her passing all those years ago when I was still a child. This experience, seeing the light and my prediction, solidified my suspicions that I had psychic abilities.

My siblings and I lived together happily for a few years until the property was sold to a shopping complex to use as a carpark. The Universe was telling me, telling all of us, that it was time to move on. It was also the ticket that I needed to secure the home I promised myself years ago. With the help of a clairvoyant, who gave me signs and a message that my father was with me spiritually,

I found the home that I knew was perfect for me. Everything that she said would be there was there.

As life went on, I eventually came face-to-face with the end of my 2 year marriage to someone I had been in a 10 year on-off relationship with. For me, the outcome was expected after I did a tarot card reading on my marriage, and the card that indicated things were not right. According to Jane Lyle's *The Lover's Tarot,* "When the Moon falls reversed it is telling you to wake up. Circumstances, in any case, may intervene and shatter your romantic idyll. The moon in this position signifies codependency, a symbiotic union in which neither partner can truly grow or flourish…. The Moon like The High Priestess, also rules what is hidden. Your partner may not be the person they seem… something or someone is undermining your relationship now… wait and see."

After the tarot reading, I waited for months to see where my marriage was going. I asked the Universe for help, to show me signs of what was happening, and to give me answers. The Universe got the memo and gave me an answer with a single phone call. The phone call I received was from a stranger—a stranger to me, but not a stranger to my husband. She exposed everything. He was living a double life, seeing a woman who was only 3 hours away and swapping wedding rings to keep up the façade.

I tried to save our marriage. We went to counselling, but that was short lived. What I discovered was it's difficult to move forward in a relationship if only one person is actively working on it. The only thing I could do was walk away.

The fallout from walking away was not easy. I felt like I had failed, like I was the problem. I went through the stages of grief. But, like always, the Universe was there for me. I realised that leaving my toxic, fake, and abusive marriage was the best thing that could happen. I had a chance to find love again. I had the time and energy to devote to myself and my ambitions. I continued to address my emotional pains and challenges, developed my tarot readings, improved my psychic and healing skills, and I found coaches and healers to teach me how to do deeper inner work.

In 2023 and 2024, I reached a turning point in my healing process. I was healing, not only my heart, but my whole ancestral family and lineage. What came up in these sessions was a generational belief that family members who were seen and heard resulted in death. With the help of the coaches and healers I worked with, I uncovered many deaths in my family history. We did everything we could to resolve and heal my family patterns.

I discovered my true soul gift through my healing journey: my ability to channel information and connect with those who have passed. In 2006, I used this gift to help my sister. We worked through her childhood pain over the phone, and I helped her prepare energetically to crossover. When she passed away in 2008, our ancestors and angels were waiting on the other side to show her the way.

What have I learned and who I am now:

My life has been filled with many unexpected and expected events, but there was no singular moment of surprise that completely turned my life around. Instead, each event in my life served as different lessons and trials that built up my understanding of The Universe, my psychic abilities, and my ability to heal my inner pain.

The Universe always has your back and wants bigger and better for you, more than you can imagine. Tarot cards and connecting to my angels and spirit guides saved me, they enabled me to connect with a power greater than me, to give me strength, courage, insight, and love. I am always guided, connected, and supported to attract miracles when I least expect them. I trust the accurate insights I receive and share them with others, offering them closure, peace, advice, and healing to go to the next level in growth and awareness.

About the Author
Di Challenor

Di Challenor's life has been marked by a series of traumatic events that left her grappling with grief and pain. Despite the overwhelming odds, Di refused to give up. She instead turned to her intuition, determined to find the hidden secrets that would allow her to break free from her past and start her healing process.

Using her innate gifts and a deep understanding of energy healing, Di was able to overcome the darkest moments of her life. She discovered that by trusting her inner voice, she could access the guidance and strength needed to overcome any challenge. Today, Di is committed to helping others by teaching them how to listen to their inner wisdom and unleash their full potential. Through her tarot card readings, channelled messages, coaching services, and healing services, she inspires others to take control of their lives and find the path to a brighter future.

Contact information :

Email: info@dichallenor.com
Facebook: https://www.facebook.com/di.challenor
Website: www.dichallenor.com

Chapter 6

Know Your Worth, Live Your Value

Elisa James

"Somehow, I lost myself," I thought as tears were pouring down my face. But how on earth did that happen? I thought I had it together. I thought I had achieved a lot in my life…

And yet, here I was on the floor, sobbing hysterically and completely out of control. I felt useless and helpless, and I knew that I would never get back the life I had known for 25 years. It was gone forever.

As I look back on that moment, almost 7 years ago now, so much has changed.

I never did get *that* version of my life back.

But what is the value of an unbalanced life?

A life where someone else is at the helm of your ship?

I know now from the benefit of hindsight, that I became that proverbial boiled frog. When you place a frog in boiling water, it will jump out. (Well, wouldn't we all?) However, if you place a frog in cold water, then put the pot on the stove, and ever so slowly turn up the heat... the frog will stay in and won't notice it is being slowly boiled to death. That's what happens to all of us when we don't **know our worth** or **stay true to our highest values.**

In my case, I was awoken from my boiled frog state about 7 years ago, after I received a shocking message from a woman telling me my husband of 25 years was a narcissist, a compulsive liar, and had compartmentalized his life for a decade. To spell it out, he had been living a double life for about 10 or more years, with four other women in tow, who all knew each other!

The poignant piece of information important to mention here is that I had just posted a picture on Facebook with the two of us having a romantic dinner at our favorite restaurant in Kansas City, Missouri. I posted how much I will miss my husband, as I was just about to fly back to Australia to visit family for a few weeks. Obviously, that post was written by a frog still in the pot...

It must have sparked great anger in the latest girlfriend because that's what instigated the private message to me.

You can only imagine the confusion, denial, shock, and embarrassment that message caused me, especially in the light of our latest romantic date night. It was all too much to take. I collapsed and went into severe shock for months.

I couldn't eat. I couldn't function. I could barely talk. I went into a completely dissociated state due to the sudden and unexpected trauma I had experienced, seemingly out of the blue.

I know what you might be thinking: "How could she not know?".

Believe me, I felt so stupid. Especially since I was one of those women who would have scoffed at this story just a few years ago and said to the woman experiencing this: "Don't be ridiculous! How could you not have known? You must have missed the signs!"

At that time, I was *supposedly* happily married and in a loving, committed relationship, so I honestly thought, "That would **never** happen to me."

It was a huge life lesson, in which, I had to take a long, hard look at everything I had thought, said, and done over the past two decades and reassess where I had gone wrong.

Just as importantly, I had to go back to the drawing board and start over.

In the months and years that followed, I studied, reflected, and grew as a person to regain my self-worth and realign with my highest values.

These words from Eleanor Roosevelt echoed in my mind:

"No one can make you feel inferior without your consent"

I would like to share with you three of the major lessons I learned during this time.

Lesson #1: Take back control of your own life! Make decisions that align with your values.

After a few months, I finally started pulling myself together again. I knew the first thing I had to do was stop judging myself (and others) and give myself some love and compassion, so I could fully heal and get back on my feet. I knew in my heart that it would take some time. I started all sorts of activities that I had never been able to do before, mostly due to my ex-husband saying "no" to my wish list.

Everything had revolved around his wishes. Mostly, because if I put my foot down and really insisted on getting my way for once, there would be hell to pay. He made sure everyone knew how angry and miserable he was to do whatever the 'thing' was. It just became easier over time to let him have his way. It meant more peace for me, however, little did I know at the time... that 'peace' came with a cost.

I had been robbing myself of my self-worth and value by letting him take control.

So, I started to do things I had always wanted to do, but never had before. I started ballroom dance lessons again, bought my first puppy, and started kickboxing, aerobics, and other fun activities.

When I started feeling a little stronger and more grounded, I hired a friend to help me take back control of my finances properly. Even though my ex-husband and I had always earned money independently of each other, my ex had taken over running the financial side of our businesses as he was simply better at it. I am embarrassed to say that I didn't even have the logins to some of our bank accounts or know where to pay monthly bills. Because of this, after our marriage came crashing down, I had no access to our banks, funding, assets, or real estate—nothing. That was one huge mistake I had to correct! And fast!

Lesson #2: Take full responsibility for your finances and stay informed, whether it be in joint accounts, mortgages, real estate, monthly bills, or whatever.

Learning how to manage my finances has been one of the most empowering lessons of my life. Though I was proficient at this during my twenties, I had simply lost touch with it after 25 years of giving up the reins during marriage.

The second real lesson about knowing my value and my worth came around a year later.

Just when I thought I had started to get my life back on track... I had yet another rude awakening that came quite unexpectedly.

In my darkest depths of despair during those first months of our separation, an old friend that I had known for more than 30 years, came back from the US and started helping me get my life back together. He helped me move out of my marital home and find a rental property on my own. He helped me get all my furniture into storage in preparation to sell it all. He helped me move into my next temporary home while I was figuring out my next move.

At first, he seemed like a gift from God. After a few months though, when I started to feel safe, I let my guard down and started a relationship with him. Over the ensuing months, he slowly became more manipulative, explosive, and even violent.

I wondered, "Why did I jump so quickly into a rebound relationship? How did I attract another male manipulator? What words and behaviors did I display to attract these types of people?"

This frog was not going to be boiled this time! Now, I was ready, willing, and able to jump out of that pot! And fast!

That opportunity came next, and it enabled me to see my life's decisions from a very different vantage point.

In fact, it was an even bigger wake-up call than the breakup with my ex.

The lesson came when my seemingly kind and helpful new 'boyfriend' had one hand over my mouth to stop me from screaming and the other hand around my neck, choking me. I honestly feared for my life. This is when I finally snapped out of my weak emotional state and was able to see what I had been blind to all those years.

I was living in fear.
Fear of being a woman alone in this world.
Fear of being unlovable.

Fear of not being enough.
Fear of....

I realized that if I had been true to my worth and truly known my value, many of these situations would not have happened.

It was time to take back control of my life!

> *"If you want to improve your self-worth,
> stop giving other people the calculator."*
> *– Tim Fargo*

As I escaped those huge hands around my neck and fled the house where we were both staying at in Italy, I knew my life was about to take a massive turn in another direction. I felt lucky to be alive and to be given another chance to rebuild, but far more carefully this time. It was either that or keep repeating the same mistakes.

So, I grabbed a bag, ran out the door, and took the first bus to nearby Venice, where I stayed in a hotel for a few days to think through the events that had led me to this point. I knew I had to choose the unknown, a higher path, a more 'solo' road for the first time in over thirty years. It was terrifying to me, but I knew I had to face the great unknown to be able to open a door to a new way of living. A life designed by me!

It only took me a day or two in Venice, alone in that hotel room, to realize that I was far stronger and more resilient than I had given myself credit for. I had to start trusting myself and give myself the chance to become the person I truly wanted to be—independent, strong, and confident in myself and my capabilities.

Lesson #3: Belief, trust, and resilience.

Nowadays, my life is very different.

Looking back, as painful as all these experiences were, they were also the best things that could have happened to me because I woke up completely and fully.

I know I will never be that boiled frog again. I had gained full control over my life, my decisions, and my finances. I run my own business. I have wonderful family and friends who love and support me. I also started to feel peaceful, happy, and free for the first time in years!

A few years later, I serendipitously met the man of my dreams. A man who allows me to be fully me, the highest and best vibration of me. He is the most kind, sweet, and compassionate human I know. He respects my values and knows my worth, just like I do. It is the most blessed and incredible feeling to know I can be truly ME every day, every minute.

When looking back at the lessons I've learned these past few years, the biggest and most inspiring one for me is knowing we are all capable of building a life and career that we love. And that's exactly what I help people do now. I help businesswomen speak with confidence and conviction, so they don't attract the wrong sorts of people into their lives.

So many women disempower themselves by the way they speak and communicate in life and business. When they undermine their authority, they lose out on opportunities for promotion, and they lose respect in the workplace. Strong women who are also feminine, confident, and articulate are sorely needed in the corporate world. I am passionate about helping businesswomen reach their full career potential by learning better speaking and communication skills.

When you communicate with calm, authentic confidence at work, you can build a career that gives you visibility and credibility in business. There is something special about a confident, capable, and happy woman. A woman who lets her voice ring out. A woman who can inspire and motivate others to change for the better.

So, ladies, know your worth, know your value. That is the first step to building authentic confidence. Once you take these steps, your life will change in positive and incredible ways you can't even imagine.

I can't wait to see what you do first!

About the Author
Elisa James M.Mus., ThM.

Elisa James is an executive voice coach, public speaking and presentation trainer, a professional actress and singer, and a best-selling author with over 40 years' experience. Elisa has a passion for teaching business communication skills and speaking performance to clients globally.

Her work focuses primarily on helping corporate leaders and small business speak and present with confidence to gain more visibility and credibility in business. She believes in a holistic approach to speaking skills – mind, body, and voice. She applies this to all her corporate workshops, coaching services, and online training programs. To book her for a corporate workshop, or arrange a free consultation regarding executive coaching services, please visit www.elisajames.com or jump over to her YouTube channel: The Voice of Confidence TV for free weekly content.

Contact information :

Website: www.elisajames.com
Youtube: The Voice of Confidence TV

Chapter 7

The Show Must Go On

Erin Coley

"Fear may simply be a call to action, a challenge to move forward despite uncertainty."
-Erin Coley

As soon as I was able to walk, living in South Florida, I would run out into the ocean, get knocked down by a wave, get up, and bolt straight back into the water. This cycle of challenge and recovery would continue until a parent ran out to save me from myself. My lack of fear terrified my caretakers.

Around the same time, my fascination with the world extended to driving. I watched every move as my mom slid her key into the car ignition and turned it. Then, one early Saturday morning, I got my mom's keys out of her purse and wandered around the house, looking for a car to drive since I was too short to reach the front door. In the corner, next to the couch, I eyed something that looked like an ignition—a power outlet! Perfect! You guessed it… I slid that key into my "ignition" and gave myself quite the shock. Doctors marveled at my survival.

Like most children, I lacked fear because I was oblivious to the potential danger stemming from my choices. I didn't realize that I could've drowned or been swept away by a wave. I obviously didn't know anything about electricity. I was simply driven by my curiosities and dreams of exploration.

Working in the theatre industry for most of my life, I've seen fear. Students in my acting programs would sometimes completely freeze up, forget all of their lines, or, in the worst case scenario, run off the stage crying hysterically. I still remember little 8-year-old Matthew in his acting showcase standing on that stage, eyes downcast, tears dripping down his chubby cheeks. As his teacher, I had to challenge him to keep going. He just had to do it. If little Matthew didn't keep going on with the show that day, he wouldn't have become the amazing actor who got into the most prestigious arts high school in South Florida and continued with a career in acting. He would've gone home and beat himself up about it for the rest of his life.

Actors and directors will tell you about "actor's nightmares" they have right before opening night. Everything goes wrong. Cast members forget their lines, the wrong music cues play, costumes malfunction, or some variation of these. Sometimes, they're in the wrong show! There are so many moving parts to a live production and it's impossible to have everything perfectly controlled. There's always room for mistakes and things inevitably go wrong. It's exciting and terrifying all at the same time, but the show always goes on. In fact, the essence of theatre is in its capacity to adapt and thrive amidst chaos.

As a first-year high school drama teacher, I remember my first directing experience. I felt inadequate and was terrified that I was going to embarrass myself. I feared the myriad of things I couldn't control—the nervous kids on the stage without a script, set pieces getting knocked over, or a student getting sick. I was afraid that something would go wrong in the middle of the show I put so much time and effort into.

We brought an act from that first show to the District Thespian Festival (a local competition for high school students). Students put up the complete set without any help from adults, and performed their play in front of students and teachers from other high schools. We had an awesome platform set with hinges so students could carry them on stage, open them, and place lids on the tops. There were a couple of stairs up to the platform. Everything looked like it was running smoothly when the last step was put in place—sideways. The unpainted backside faced the audience, and nothing but the decorative, thin wood facing was on the top. There wasn't enough time to run backstage, stop the show, and fix the set piece. So, we sat in the audience, chewing on our fingers until, inevitably, the first student stepped on the step and their foot crashed straight down to the stage floor. Luckily, no one was hurt, and each of those students learned a valuable lesson about persevering through obstacles when the show went on.

That fear was compounded when my own children were on stage. As my son flew over the stage as Peter Pan, I worried that the rope would snap and he would come tumbling to the ground. What if they messed up? What if, even worse, they froze in fear?

Now, after hundreds of shows, I still get excited, but my perspective on fear has changed. I know that things inevitably WILL go wrong. I also know that "the show must go on," and it does. Believe it or not, over the 30+ years I've seen and done theatre, I've never stopped a production because things got too out of control. I've sat with the awkward audience while students struggle with their next line or skip entire scenes. I've seen missed light and sound cues, lost props, and even broken sets.

Our fears stem from things we can't control and our imaginations concocting a "worst case scenario." Fear isn't always bad. Sometimes it simply does what it's intended to do—keep us out of danger. Other times, it's a reminder to focus on something important.

When my students have a big project, speech, or audition coming up, I always ask how they feel. When they say they are nervous, I smile and reply, "Good. Nerves mean you care about what you are doing."

If nerves are simply an early version of fear, then is fear a bad thing? At what point do the nerves get so powerful that they become debilitating fear? When do they move from being a positive thing to a negative thing?

The first time I remember feeling true fear was when I was 25 years old. I had been skydiving on and off for about seven years. My mom and dad were both skydivers, but they didn't let me go on my first jump until I was 18. At 25, I was a single mom with two very young children. For the first time, as I held onto the edge of the airplane door frame, looking down at the blur of ground, I felt this strange sensation. I didn't want to jump. I wasn't scared of getting hurt. I was afraid of leaving my children without a mom. I suddenly realized that my carelessness and need for that adrenaline rush could essentially affect people I love in a negative way. I still jumped that day, but it was my last jump. Fear, in this instance, was what it was intended to be—a red light, or at least a yellow one.

Right before my 24th birthday and 5 months pregnant, I made the difficult choice to leave my husband of four years. I took my 21-month-old son and my rapidly growing belly and drove cross-country from New Mexico to South Florida. I was nervous about supporting my growing family, but I knew I had no other option. I had to make it work. And make it work, I did. I worked multiple jobs and took 27 college credit hours at one time (12 credits was considered a full load). I juggled school, work, single-parenthood, and my new life, and didn't have time to think about it.

Perhaps this was when I realized that the best way for the show to go on was by moving on, one step at a time. While skydiving and leaving a marriage were terrifying, they were also catalysts for change. They pushed me toward a future shaped by my actions rather than my apprehensions.

I guess that's why I balk when people ask me how I was able to sell my house and business, jump into an RV, and travel for three years. I don't remember feeling fear. As soon as the wheels were in motion, I was simply excited. I couldn't wait to do what I always dreamed of doing—travel while teaching. We spent three full years exploring 42 states and 5 countries, and they were the best years of my life.

There's a moment immediately after recognizing fear when you have a decision to make. Most experts have named the choices as "fight or flight." You can fight the thing that is causing fear, or you can run away from it. This makes sense in a lot of instances, but I like to look at our fear responses through the lens of action. Fear may simply be a call to action, a challenge to move forward despite uncertainty.

The only thing keeping us from finding joy is inaction. The fear that causes us to freeze, stop, quit, and fly away is the reason there aren't more Taylor Swifts, Steve Jobs, Leonardo da Vincis, and Michael Jordans in the world. Every one of us has the untapped talent to be that successful in something. The only thing holding us back from it is the fear of the next step—the fear of taking action. We must move forward into the unknown, scary future. We must take action. But how? How does one break free from the fear that causes inaction and take action?

The fear of what's next is what makes us hesitate, sometimes permanently. In our minds, we tend to imagine that there is a scary monster or deep pit around that dark corner because we can't see the next step. Our imaginations consider the worst possible scenario, and we freeze in inaction. If we don't move forward, we won't be disappointed, we won't be in danger, and we won't be hurt. So instead, we wait until the next step is illuminated by someone or something, which usually never comes. In the meantime, the wind blows us to something else that is easier, clearer, and has less resistance.

When it comes to our dreams, goals, and resolutions, we will inevitably hit this dark and scary next step at some point. Everyone does, and it's why the typical 90%-98% of the world will never get to where they want to be.[1] Fear of that next step causes us to freeze in inaction.

So how do we counteract that fear that leads to inaction?

Imagine a trail where you are being chased by a lion. You come across a dark, rickety bridge, and you hesitate. You look over your shoulder and see that lion approaching quickly. You weigh your two options, and you step out onto that bridge. You have no idea whether it will hold you or where it leads, but the alternative is being eaten by a hungry lion. In essence, you have no other choice. You have to go.

When I left my first husband, I knew that the option of staying was dangerous and much scarier than what lay ahead. When I sold everything and moved into an RV, I knew I didn't want to work myself to death for the rest of my life. I knew I wanted something different, something better.

The moment before an actor walks onto a stage, there's a moment where they look out at that dark, scary audience and have no idea how they will be perceived or if they even have what it takes to be successful out there. Their alternative is standing in the wings, watching the show go on without them.

What scary thing is behind you, chasing you? What are your scary alternatives? Stop focusing on the imagined scary thing in front of you and consider what your life will look like if you do nothing, if you take no action, and if you stay where you are right now. Is this what you really want? If so, great! Chances are that you already made some tough moves that got you to the content place you are right now. If not, life is moving forward. The clock is ticking. The time is now.

Once you identify the "lion" behind you, the thing you want to move away from, fear that and step onto the bridge. Be afraid of the danger of returning to it. When you feel stuck, imagine that it's getting closer, and you must move now into the unknown future.

Ultimately, the challenges we face and the fears we overcome are what define us. They remind us that the essence of life is not in avoiding risk but in embracing it, learning from it, and moving forward with courage, focus, and determination. In doing so, we become part of the rare few who dare to step out of the shadows of fear and into the light of their potential, proving that the show will go on, with or without us.

---

[1]*Failory.com 2022, University of Scranton 2016, National Collegiate Athletic Association 2020*

About the Author
Erin Coley

Erin Coley, M.Ed., is a dynamic communication and theatre expert, entrepreneur, and transformative coach. With a keen focus on breaking barriers, she excels in guiding both children and adults to surpass their limitations by embracing growth through deliberate challenges. Erin's innovative approach in coaching, along with her impactful workshops and classes, have propelled thousands toward achieving their aspirations in all things communication - acting, public speaking, writing, and beyond. As a visionary, she co-founded Standing Ovation Performing Arts, TE3N Empowerment, and Coley Productions, empowering thousands of students along the way.

Outside her mission of transformation, Erin finds joy in poker, pickleball, and hikes to waterfalls. A mother of four and wife of 22 years, she recently made her home in Las Vegas, Nevada, after three years of traveling in an RV across the world. For a deeper connection or to embark on your journey of self-improvement, visit her website.

Contact information :

Website: www.erincoley.com

Chapter 8

Fear Never Visits Just Once

Suellen Brook

Receiving the news was terrifying.

I had only three weeks to make a final decision that would alter the life of my 6-year-old daughter forever. She needed brain surgery, and I was the one that had to sign off on its approval. It's not as if I had a choice in the matter. Of course, she needed the surgery. Of course, I was going to sign off on it. But the weight of that decision, knowing it was necessary but also risky, haunted me.

The gravity of it all was overwhelming—another significant burden I could scarcely bear. The impulse to escape, to reject, and to rebel against this harsh turn of events consumed me. Pain, fear, and uncertainty became intense, as if it were a relentless predator gnawing at my heart. I found myself in a state of despair, overcome with fear, and searching desperately for an exit. I wanted to run, fight, cry, and scream all at once. Yet none of it was working. None of my emotional upheavals were going to alter the situation we were confronted with.

To understand the depth of my situation, let me start the story from the beginning.

When my daughter, Shannon, was still just a baby of only 6 weeks, her doctor diagnosed her with NF1. Neurofibromatosis type 1—a term as unfamiliar as it was alarming. He noticed multiple "café au lait" spots on her belly, named for their light coffee colour, as well as some freckling under her armpits. This genetic disorder affects the nervous system and leads to the growth of non-cancerous tumours around nerve endings. It wasn't the non-cancerous nature of the tumours that frightened me; it was their potential locations.

The diagnosis was startling, particularly because this condition was not previously known to be present in our family. We knew that she would need to be monitored for any changes, but we were oblivious to the changes that were to come. The uncertainty of the situation was the most dreadful aspect, casting a dark and unknown shadow over us.

I didn't have time to grieve. I had to stay strong for her, to be the rock that she and the rest of my family needed. There were three children in this household; the third was her father, my husband. Shackled by PTSD, there was little conversation; he was closed off from friends, family, and especially me. My husbands PTSD created his negative demeanour and energy, which I had come to despise. For years, I had lived daily with someone who resembled a walking, heavy blanket that was completely lifeless. His presence in our lives and through Shannon's journey made everything more difficult.

Despite how difficult life was with my husband, our daughter grew up like any other child. She was happy, curious, gentle, and loving. Due to having low muscle tone, she went to physiotherapy and speech therapy. She learned how to swim, excelled in school, and was loved by her friends and family—just a beautiful child.

When Shannon was 6 years old, as a mum, I noticed that she was showing the early signs of puberty. She had pubic hair beginning to grow and small breast buds appearing. I was concerned, so I took her to see her doctor.

Her paediatrician agreed that something was not quite adding up after her blood test came back with no abnormal activity. Her paediatrician sent me away with a form for an MRI of her brain.

On Monday, five days later, she was inside the MRI. At this time, MRIs were the latest high-tech machines used for soft tissue imaging. At 32-years-old, I had never heard of this big, noisy clanking machine before. It surrounded her inside its core with its hideous sound, and on and on it banged to its own tune. Near my breaking point, I had to leave the room and get outside of its tense grip.

That same week, on Wednesday, I left for work, following my usual routine. It started mundanely, like any other day in September 1999. I dropped the children off at school, then went to the secondary school I taught at.

A school staff member came to my door in the morning with a note saying, "The paediatrician has asked for you to ring him back."

"Oh, ok," I said as I took the note.

I called him during lunch, but a nurse answered the line instead. She calmly relayed, "Your daughter's doctor would like to see you and your child this afternoon at approximately 6:00 p.m."

"Tonight?"

"Yes, tonight."

My gut instinct went into overdrive. No one gets a phone call from the paediatric surgery department to see them after hours without a good reason.

I hung up the phone, but the rest of the day was spent in deep worry and questions that flooded my mind: "What did they find or not find? Why was the doctor calling me? Was the news bad or good?"

Over and over, the thoughts played, and over and over, I was left without answers until I finally arrived to see the doctor in Nambour (Australia). As soon as we arrived, he called us and took us to one of the rooms in the back. Ever so slowly and quietly, he pulled out the MRI results. His face grew grim at what he saw before he finally spoke. "We have an answer; it isn't just the hormones. Shannon will need to see a neurosurgeon ASAP at the Royal Children's Hospital as this tumour is also growing through the optic nerves in both of her eyes."

He showed me the scan and pointed out the issue. There was a golf ball-sized white tumour sitting just above her pituitary gland, which was irritating it. The tumour was also the cause of her early onset puberty.

The doctor explained then that her eyesight was being affected, but an investigation was needed to find out the extent. It wasn't her eyes as such, but the nerves behind them that gave the brain visual information. These nerves were irreparable, and the damage was irreversible.

My stomach and heart both dropped and fell to the floor, just another reaction to fear and the unknown. I had to breathe in and draw on every small bit of fibre within my body and my past to hold back the floodgate of tears.

Two days later, we arrived at the Royal Children's Hospital in Brisbane. The severity and enormity of the situation kicked in. I had dealt with fear all my life, but this was different. The fear was not for myself, but for my daughter. On the inside, I was a mess. I was trying my best to keep Shannon calm by reading stories, while the heavy blanket (my husband) sat in silence.

The neurosurgeon walked us to his room. He left for a moment, then quickly returned with news, "We can operate on Shannon in three weeks."

"What?! You want me to give you permission to go into my daughter's head in three weeks?!" I responded in exasperation, followed by, "And what if I don't give you permission?"

"The tumour will continue to grow, and she will go blind," the doctor stated.

After a long 2 hour drive home, I took the children into the lounge room.

"Shanny, the doctors are concerned about a lump that is growing in your brain, and they are worried that if they don't do something soon, it might affect your eyes."

"Does that mean I won't be able to see you, mum?"

That question pierced my heart like a searing knife.

"Of course, they just need to do an operation to take it out."

The following three weeks were nothing but emotional torture. Fear of the unknown had wormed into my skin, throughout my body, and consumed my brain.

For the next three weeks, I found solace by sitting on the ride-on mower. There was something soothing about it that helped to calm my nerves—the noise, the repetition, the escape from being trapped indoors. It was the only comfort I had as I struggled to function.

I wasn't hungry.
I wasn't sleeping.
I wanted to vomit.
I wanted to scream.
I wanted all of this to go away.

I wanted true support from my husband.
I wanted 'normal' back.

My life was out of control, and my daughter's would soon be out of my hands.

After three weeks, we arrived at the Royal Children's Hospital and made our way to the operating theatre. To see Shannon in a surgical gown as the nurse walked her towards the preparation room was gut wrenching.

Her surgery was the longest six hours of my life.

I was emotionally and physically exhausted.

The light had faded. Waiting. There was no sign of life. No footsteps. Nothing. Sterile. Lonely.

After 8 p.m., her surgeon arrived. "I am happy with what we have done. We have debulked the tumour as much as we can. I am sending a sample to pathology as I expect it to be benign, but I can't rule out that it isn't. More tests will need to be done to determine what she may be able to see," the doctor responded. It turns out the tumour was benign.

In the ICU, Shannon was peaceful, her face swollen, and her head heavily bandaged. She had a titanium plate securing her head and 36 staples holding the skin around her face. There were drips and heart and BP monitors.

At 9 a.m., Shannon opened her eyes, and coherently asked for a Pepsi and a doughnut for breakfast!

My fear was released.

There was a noise and movement to the left of me. The heavy blanket had grabbed a container and was vomiting. The vomiting was hideously symbolic of what I had dealt with for two years. A man who had checked out on his child and on all of us. Everything yet again fell on my shoulders; my little girl needed me, but that didn't mean I wasn't afraid.

Fear has been a constant in my life.

I was the only child of five to survive, and I was forced to live as all of them. I was the responsible, high achieving child. I stood in front of people making speeches, singing, dancing, riding horses, playing piano in concerts, and achieving an award from Queen Elizabeth II. You can only imagine the pressure I was under and the fear I constantly faced before each event.

When my mother went through her diabetic episodes, I had to grab the wheel from her hands and steer us back to the road. Fear was a jolt, but momentary.

The heavy blanket I called a husband was suicidal and refused help. I spent years living with the fear that he would take his life, or worse, that my children would be around to witness it. Ten years after Shannon's surgery, we finally divorced.

Over and over again, fear knocked and shattered my soul. It spun me out of control. I had to face it head on and control it. I drew upon everything I had learned from my childhood: to be rational and steadfastly strong, and to have faith that everything would be okay.

I regarded fear as its own entity and life as a chessboard. I was in control of the board and the pieces, and played fear on my own terms. I had to take back my control. I went back to work full-time. On my days off, I went to the gym and the beach to regain my fitness and strengthen my mind. I would not let fear control me.

My journey with Shannon still continues since her condition is progressive. She's now 30, is legally blind but still able to see, works part time, and is very independent. We've had so many scares over the years, but I learned that fear does not control me. Fear is a choice. Fear doesn't know how strong you really are!

About the Author
Suellen Brook

Suellen Brook currently lives on the Sunshine Coast, Qld Australia, with her adult daughter, 5 horses, 2 dogs and 2 cats. Suellen is a state and national show horse judge. She facilitates equine-assisted learning and therapy, is a fully registered teacher of students with special needs, and CPDs in the mental health of children and adults.

Currently, she also works as a coach on life and mindset as part of her business. She is an NLP Master Practitioner and a Time Line Master Therapist. She is also a keynote speaker on a variety of topics.

Suellen has written 3 children's books that focus on teaching children life lessons based on the antics of the horses and dogs on her property.

This is her first exciting adventure collaborating on a book with other authors.

Contact Information

Email:

info@positivepathway.com.au

FB Page:

https://www.facebook.com/positivepathwaylifeskills/

Facebook:

https://www.facebook.com/suellen.brook.7

(Mindset Coaching)

Website/ Join us!:

https://www.positivepathway.com.au/lead-collection

(Mindset Coaching)

Website:

https://www.positivepathway.com.au/

(Equine Assisted Therapy/ Life skills)

Chapter 9

Embracing Fear, Finding Inner Strength

Irene Gathuru

*"Confront fear to uncover one's true identity
and purpose in your journey of self-discovery."*
-Irene Gathuru

As I stood at the Costco checkout, groceries piled in my cart, I confidently handed over my debit card, expecting a smooth transaction. However, my confidence quickly dissipated as the cashier's expression turned from polite impatience to concern when my card was declined. Frustrated and anxious, I hurriedly opened my banking app, hoping to find an error. Instead, I was faced with the harsh truth, leaving me sheepishly whispering an apology. I left behind my shopping cart and exited the store with a confident demeanor, only to break down in tears once I reached the privacy of my car.

It was the year 2019, a period that I would always remember as a terrible time. Financially, I was facing unprecedented challenges.

Opportunities that used to come easily were no longer available. I was determined to keep trying, sending out my resume with the hope of finding a job. However, despite my unwavering effort, I kept finding myself right back where I started.

As the year came to an end, our debts appeared insurmountable, like an imposing mountain. It started with the loss of our cars. The first car was repossessed, and the other car was wrecked. Our credit scores dropped, guaranteeing a future of relying on borrowed transportation and public transit. The final blow was the eviction notice.

My family's financial standing was undeniably dismal, especially when compared to that of other families at the independent preparatory school my son attended. I remember him commenting with astonishment that one of his schoolmates wore a $500 belt to school. I felt ashamed that my son was living the prince and pauper tale. My heart ached for him as I wondered how he was processing what was happening in our family. I would not have blamed him if he had decided to dissociate himself from me while on the campus grounds. This stark contrast at my son's school forced me to examine my life. I realized that fear was always with me, pushing me to seek perfection in the pursuit of a flawless life.

I grew up with a lot of praise for my good behavior and strong academic performance, and this attention was alluring. I did all that I could to keep this attention on me by doing more of the same thing. As I got older, fear had a progressively stronger grip on me, and the thought of failure made me shudder. I started experiencing panic attacks in school, and taking tests began to feel like a do-or-die situation. To ease the pressure to maintain impeccable academic performance, I perfected the art of playing it safe, never wavering from the path I thought would bring me success and validation.

The blueprint that I had followed—go to school, get good grades, and get a great job—was no longer working for me. This detour from my path to success left me feeling lost as I was now in uncharted territory. I began to question my own identity and purpose. But with the eviction that was looming, I went into survival mode by doing everything I could to get the bills paid in full.

What I experienced next felt even worse than my fear of failure. It was the shame that I felt about my dire financial situation. Almost twenty years earlier, I had earned my Ph.D. in Public Health, and I never would have guessed that my life would take such an ugly turn. I asked myself how I had allowed myself to go from the pinnacle of academic success to the depths of financial distress. I had a lot of soul-searching to do.

As I reflected on my childhood, I had an epiphany. For as long as I can remember, I have always been a daydreamer. I escaped the boredom of living on a farm by spending my waking hours engrossed in reading encyclopedias and indulging in visualization of myself as a globetrotter. My daydreaming also helped me to cope with painful and traumatic experiences. My circumstances made me realize how much the escapism was holding me back from taking ownership of my life. And now, I could no longer escape this brutal truth.

Although all our accounts in arrears were paid in full after six months, I wanted to understand how two decades ago I had earned a Ph.D. with a bright future to becoming a broke and underemploye person with no sight of the promising future that I had envisioned for myself. So, I went on a journey of personal development and got hooked on this subject.

As I was reading Brene Brown's book, *The Gifts of Imperfection*, I came across a passage that forever changed my viewpoint of the life that I had led. There it was, on page 56, under Perfectionism:

"... Most perfectionists were raised being praised for achievement and performance (grades, manners, rule-following, people-pleasing, appearance, sports). Somewhere along the way, we adopt this dangerous and debilitating belief system: I am what I accomplish and how well I accomplish it..."

I read this passage over and over again, and I was overcome with tears of joy.

It all made sense. I have lived all my life thinking that there was something wrong with me. This was not true. I discovered that I was not the only one on planet Earth who was a prisoner of fear. Now I wondered: How many opportunities had I missed? How many times had I played small? How many times did I beat myself up because I did not feel good enough? I was so angry with myself, but I was feeling weary from all the heaviness that I had hauled around like luggage.

Behind the mask that I wore, I was tormented by these thoughts. I refrained from talking about these deeply seated feelings and thoughts because of the shame that I carried and the fear of abandonment if people knew how pathetic I really was. I had been reluctant to be introspective. So, to ease the pain, my mind wandered into oblivion, into the make-believe world about the joyful life that I would live as a heart-centered globetrotter who was a visionary. I had been leading a life in which events took place by happenstance, not by design. My current life did not reflect that I was following my passion.

I knew something had to change if I wanted to take my last breath without regret, knowing that I had led a joyful and fulfilled life. This thought was sobering and became a goal to strive for.

To live the life I wanted, I recalled a concept I had heard of but never applied—an alter ego. I thought it was intriguing but too "woo-woo" for me. With what had transpired in my life, it was time to do something different if I was going to die without having regret. Just like Clarke Kent becomes Superman when he wears a cape, I created an alter ego but without a cape. My alter ego was my secret identity that I would now use to change the course of my life.

My alter ego would stand in for Irene as the heroine to overcome the false beliefs that Irene had accepted about herself, about her worth, and about her abilities. The heroine was kind, compassionate, and nonjudgmental. She knew Irene as a misguided but well-meaning woman, who was motivated by fear and avoidance of what she did not want in her life. Irene was too afraid to get into the ring, stand out, and fight for what she stood for. The self-loathing had to stop. In its place, self-forgiveness and self-compassion were to be embraced.

This has been and continues to be a life-changing shift in mindset since I started using a heroine to help me overcome my false beliefs, unrealistic expectations of perfection, and self-doubt. I have learned that bravery comes from taking action despite feeling fearful. Self-confidence is gained through keeping commitments that I make to myself, and what I thought of as failure is indeed feedback on what changes I need to make in my life.

My life continues to evolve as I gain confidence in stepping into the realm of uncertainty and taking action, even when I feel fearful. After years of struggling to get back into the field of public health, it was a relief to let go. It was difficult to do because my identity had been wrapped around this field. As I explored different types of businesses to find one that resonated with me, I was inspired by many businesswomen. I learned that success is achieved by taking deliberate actions despite fear and self-doubt. I also learned that I needed to be authentic and vulnerable to build genuine connections with other people.

As far as my personal growth and development, I learned the secret to creating habits that stick. I heard the following expression among businesswomen: "Be, do, have." First, we decide on what we want to have or get. Second, envision the qualities of the person who will get the results that we want. Lastly, we take the actions that they would take to get the desired outcome.

With this newfound understanding, I realigned my career path and embraced my challenges as integral to my life's purpose. Instead of holding onto a victim mentality, I am now committed to helping empty nest moms navigate their transformations as they create their "Champion Chapter" with a focus on their own goals and dreams. By adopting the appropriate mindset, reshaping one's identity becomes crucial for attaining enduring success.

The Five Lessons I Learned Along My Journey

1. Pay attention to your blind spots regarding how you deal with fear. They will impact the meaning of what is happening in your life, the decisions you make, and the actions you take.

2. Be vulnerable and share your journey with others. There is power in discovering that there are others who have similar experiences. They normalize your experience to give you a fresh perspective on how to forge a new or different path to create the life you desire.

3. The lessons that you learn during the times you miss the mark or don't get the results you want are pivotal for creating the breakthrough for your transformation.

4. Adopt the idea of an alter ego to overcome false beliefs about your abilities, limitations, and resourcefulness. Lean in on this identity to create empowering self-talk and push through your fear that may masquerade as procrastination, perfectionism, self-doubt, indecision, or overthinking.

5. There is no breakthrough or growth without adversity. Without confronting our fears, there will be stagnation in life.

About the Author
Irene Gathuru

Irene Gathuru, a midlife coach, is passionate about guiding empty nest moms to prioritize self-care and envision their future goals in order to create a fulfilling next stage in their lives, which she refers to as their "Champion Chapter." As a married mother of two sons, who are currently in college, Irene draws from her extensive experience as a health researcher and former roles as a childbirth educator, health educator, grant writer, and education advocate. She is also a dedicated supporter of grassroots initiatives for women, youth, and children.

In her free time, Irene enjoys exploring her culinary skills, indulging in literature, immersing herself in music, attending cultural events, traveling, and staying informed about health and wellness. She has a PhD in Epidemiology and an MPH in Behavioral and Community Health Sciences.

Contact information :

Facebook: https://www.facebook.com/irene.gathuru/
LinkedIn: https://linkedin.com/in/irenegathuru/

Chapter 10

Embracing the Journey: From Fear to Freedom

Jaisha Rose

Growing up, people always asked me, "Could you please do my hair and makeup? You would make a great hairstylist!"

Growing up, I've declined many requests, but the few I've accepted came with great compliments. Unfortunately, I'd turn those great compliments into harsh critiques of my own work. I'd speak so negatively about the work I did, the hair that made someone feel like a new person, and the makeup that boosted self-confidence. My work was truly admired, but I did not deserve such praise. Admiration would only inspire hope; the hope that I had known all too well would lead to disappointment when, not if, things did not work out.

Growing up, I perceived being a hairstylist as the "typical" profession for someone such as myself, but was it really? And why did I view being a hairstylist as only "typical"? Could I, ME, make it something more? Back then, I never believed it. I was certain I was someone who would never succumb to being just "typical."

I've strayed away from the ideal "normal" for years. I have a huge personality that can only be described as "eccentrically obnoxious," or, in other words, someone who stands out, and I very much stood out in the way I did my hair, my makeup, the way I dressed, and the way I carried myself. I was far from being just "normal." Ironically, I worked in retail management through most of my adulthood. Try as I might to pursue anything else, my social nature always led me to one dead end retail job after the next. Though the pay was good, I was never truly happy. Between these jobs, I dabbled in hair, makeup, and costumes. It was the only thing that seemed to bring me genuine excitement.

It took many years before I finally realized I had been pursuing my calling THE ENTIRE TIME! Anytime I did hair and makeup for shows, weddings, special occasions, or even on myself, I was pursuing what my heart had always longed for: a creative outlet to be more than the "typical," more than the "normal." Despite my life's purpose, which I had denied for decades. I used the excuse that being a hairstylist or beautician was too "typical" for someone like me, but the fact of the matter is, I was too afraid to even try. What if I failed? What if I wasn't good enough?

My fear kept me locked in the mediocrity and dissatisfaction that was my life until I finally hit an all-time low. Corporate life completely drained me. It was exhausting being fake all the time with the constant parrot replies of: "Yes, ma'am. No, ma'am. Yes, sir. No, sir." I was tired of conforming to what the world believed was "ideal" and tired of investing my all just to be continuously overlooked. My spirit yearned for more.

The weight of my misery kept me pinned, leading to a long chat with my sister in hopes of finding some direction. Her suggestion – beauty school. This time her reply was more than just a casual conversation or a nonchalant nudge; she truly did believe I could do and be more. She had just gone through a transformation of her own, and its fruits were starting to show. Even so, my first reaction to her suggestion was, "Ugh, absolutely not!" I've never doubted her sincerity, and it wasn't the first time she told me to pursue cosmetology. Many family and friends, even strangers, tried to convince me to pursue this path, but again, "typical" kept playing in the back of my mind. My biggest fears began to surface at the thought of her suggestion, leaving anxiety to take over once again.

Over the next few days, I thought hard about what she had said. I had so many reasons not to do this, all of them rooted in fear and excuses. "What if I fail? What if I'm not good enough? What if I'm viewed as just 'typical' when they find out who I am? What if…what if…" These thoughts played over and over in my mind.

Eventually, like any other song that plays on repeat for too long, I got tired of the music, and the lyrics turned into white noise. This left room for new thoughts: "I'm already at rock bottom. I might as well give this a try. Things couldn't possibly get worse."

And that was it. I made my decision.

I quit my job, sold my car, packed my bags, and flew back to a place I once called home – "Sin City" – Las Vegas, Nevada. As I sat on the plane, dreaming of my new life, mostly the many things that could go wrong, I thought to myself, "Damn! I'm really doing this! I'm really pursuing the 'typical' profession! I'm seriously moving to Vegas! There's no way any of this can be real!" It became very real as hours passed, with the ocean turning into farmland, and farmland turning into the infamous casinos that lined the Vegas Strip. Yup!! It was real!

Doubts turned over and over in my head as I stepped off the plane. I felt sick. I thought with time it would go away. I believed I would be better. Self-doubt replaced misery as the weight that pulled me down. Fear of the unknown and fear of not being enough were friends of self-doubt that often hung around at the worst of times. I found myself drowning under their words. I did what I could to stay afloat, but it was a struggle. A struggle that almost led me to drop out of beauty school because I was terrified my thoughts would push me to failure.

Survival is what kept me afloat long enough for me to discover a belief in my abilities and the realization that I was good enough—more than good enough—to pursue cosmetology. If only I had listened back then to the words of my loved ones when they told me I had talent. To me, those songs of praise were biased. Of course, they would say I was great. It took the words of strangers—people who I never met—to validate the truth that I was and am truly amazing at my craft. Even so, I found such kindness hard to believe. Self-doubt tried time and time again to sabotage my confidence, but I prevailed. I reminded myself that I have, can, and will accomplish many great achievements as a stylist and beautician. All I had to do was be patient, work hard, and give it a fair shot.

While in beauty school, I've had many freelance jobs doing what? Hair and makeup! As I got further into beauty school and graduated, I was blessed with greater opportunities to do hair and makeup for Cirque Du Solei, the Billboard Awards, work on music videos, do Halloween hair and makeup for Dana White's family, and so on. These validating accomplishments really kept me focused on the end prize. Throughout my time in beauty school, I've won first place in every hair and makeup competition held. With each victory, self-doubt quieted down. I proved to myself that the lies my fears created were just that—lies.

However, beauty school was only a brief chapter in what was to come. Once I graduated, I would no longer be able to fall on the excuse of being just a student when I made mistakes. I would have to take accountability for my work, whether good or bad, both were my responsibility. I should have been terrified. The route to being a professional beautician is daunting—filled with failure, higher expectations, demanding hours, the need to build contacts and networks, acquiring a workspace and equipment, and so much more that I was unaware of until I graduated. The thought of these things left me anxious but no longer fearful. In the same way we get anxious about what comes next in a movie, it's the same way I felt about my future as a beautician. I didn't know entirely what to expect.

After I graduated from beauty school, I decided that I would do the only logical thing and work for myself. I couldn't stomach the idea of answering to someone else again or working my way up from the bottom. Being my own boss would give me the freedom I always wanted. I was able to set my own schedule, pick my own customers, and make a shop that I could work in comfortably. There was just one tiny problem with this dream: I had no idea how to start or run a business. Luckily, the family that always believed in me provided me with all the steps, materials, and information that I needed to finally live the life I've always dreamed of. All I needed to do now was follow through, and follow through I did with numerous achievements, several high-profile clients, many events, and an endless list of extremely satisfied customers.

My journey to becoming a hairstylist is only a small fraction of my life, but it remains the biggest change I've ever faced and overcame. Self-doubt and fear were the greatest aggressors on this path and held me back from pursuing my dream for so long, but I was able to silence them by taking a chance and proving that I could be more. It wasn't for anyone else but myself.

I found out that I am far more capable than I once thought I was, if I just took a risk and tried. Trying, even if there are moments of failure, is necessary to make anything happen. I vowed to myself that no matter what may come, no matter the thoughts or circumstances, I will always try. If I did not take the chance of leaving my old life, if I did not put in the effort in school, and if I never attempted to open my own business by simply trying, I know I would not be where I am today.

Life is all about the journey, taking the risk, and facing the challenge head on. I've released my self-saboteur, but more importantly, being a transwoman, I absolutely love and embrace this extra-ordinarily "typical" career path that has been laid out in front of me all along.

When embarking on your own journey, you must take risks while remaining true to yourself. As the beautiful Coco Chanel said, "Beauty begins the moment you decide to be yourself."

About the Author
Jaisha Rose

Jaisha Rose is a forward-thinking hairstylist who has transformed the beauty industry with her unique vision and creativity. Jaisha's profound passion for beauty emerged from her dominant character. Encouraged by her family, she made the life-altering choice to enroll in beauty school in Las Vegas, Nevada.

Jaisha's career took a dramatic shift when she began taking on freelance jobs. From styling hair for Cirque Du Soleil to working at the Billboard Awards, she found herself gaining significant opportunities.

Jaisha is a self-reliant stylist and artist who has journeyed globally to assist in the transformation of individuals, whether through a haircut or the application of makeup that holds significant meaning in the creation of a new identity.

Contact information :

Instagram: @Jaisha357

Chapter 11

From "When" to "How"

Simonne Liley

"Are you scared of dying?" I asked.

I was visiting my brother, who had been given a six-month terminal diagnosis just two months earlier. We were driving to the second cemetery of the day to choose his resting place.

"I'm scared of facing Jesus," he replied. He had a strong faith and ministered in his younger days, so I wasn't surprised.

"Oh right, yeah, because of having had affairs?" I asked.

"No, not at all. I'm scared because I forsook him in that period of my life."

As was common when my brother and I spoke, there was a pregnant pause as we both processed what had just been said.

Despite living in a different country, I saw my brother many times in the next few months. I was gifted with raw conversations about thoughts and topics that many people never get the opportunity to have, particularly with someone facing the ultimate deadline—no pun intended. I put my business on hold, limited my contracts, and spent as much time as I could with my brother. We were each other's confidante, cheerleader, and support in a somewhat colourful family dynamic.

Ironically, on Good Friday, a fall at home put him into a coma. He came back into consciousness on Sunday for several hours as though nothing had happened.

"Swanee! How come you're here?" he asked excitedly when he saw me.

We were all gifted with a glimpse of the man that he was until that evening, when he lost consciousness again, taking his final breath on Monday afternoon.

We'd spoken regularly. Often sharing our past, our experiences, our thoughts on philosophy and life theory, our failings and fears, our learnings and loves, and our dreams. Big, big dreams—to make an impact and make the money to live a life of freedom and possibilities.

The word "when" was always in our conversation: when the children are older, when I have more time, when I've lost weight, or when I have more money.

It was always "when" anything occurred that we would finally take action, but "when" never really occurred. The question of "when" became more distant as life got in the way. Besides, who were we to have such grand dreams in the first place?

When my brother passed, there was a stark realisation that he never got his "when." There was an even starker realisation that, if I continued doing what I was doing, I wouldn't either.

My brother was 56, and I was 50. I had six years to turn my "when" into anything! I was determined to make his life count and to make a difference in the world. Up until now, I'd made more excuses than impact. It was time to stop waiting for the "when" and start taking action towards my goals. My brother's passing served as a wake-up call to live with purpose and intention.

However, changing my life was easier said than done. If I wanted to change, I had to start by confronting my past and embracing who I was, my decisions, my experiences, and everything that I once believed.

I was born into my family by purpose: to secure a future for a frightened and wounded mother. While her future was secured, mine was not. My childhood was filled with abuse and torture, reminding me constantly that I was never enough. I was always in the wrong place at the wrong time, never wanted and never needed.

By high school, my daily routine was to stand under the vodka bowser, swallowing two or three shots, as I passed through the house bar on my way out the front to catch the school bus. Along with the drinking, I turned to pills. The pills my mother left behind some years earlier, when she'd left to secure another future with another man. I kept her cocktail of unmarked pills wrapped in a tissue and secured in the pocket of my second-hand uniform. It was my insurance if I felt like today was the day that it was all too much.

From the outside, my life seemed normal. People thought I was lucky, even spoiled. They believed that the blueprint of my life was laid out perfectly for me, they couldn't be more wrong. I was debilitated with low self-esteem, making one bad choice after another. I was looking for the love I couldn't feel for myself outside of me and in all the wrong places—in men who didn't mean what they said or discarded me as I deserved. It became normal to feel numb; to expect anything more, was a fairytale.

I deeply believed what I was told—too sensitive, damaged goods, broken.

While I was numb to myself, I was not numb to the world. I lay awake at night and heard the wounded and the hurting. I could hear and feel their untold stories, their pain, and their gorgeous truth. That's the price of being sensitive.

My deepest wish was to invent a pill. A pill, just like I used to have in my high school uniform. A pill to take the pain away and immediately give you self-confidence. How could I invent such a thing? How could I find that elusive piece of the puzzle?

Life held more bad choices with some good and some self-development. I read a book here and there, and attended a course or two. I told myself that when I get enough money, I'll do more. I volunteered to work with rape crisis, seeking counselling and growth, and confronting and reconciling with some of my abusers. I went through a divorce, had two incredible children, and started a business.

However, having put my life on hold and always putting myself second, I found myself in a financial bind. Imagine the shame of telling people that I, an accountant, was planning to file for bankruptcy. I had no idea how I was going to get out of this, but I knew I had to figure it out.

Out of the blue, I received an email from a coach that I had wanted to work with the previous year, but due to my finances, I was unable to. He was offering a three-day event in Sydney. These were great events, full of tools and inspiration, with a ticket price of around A$3000 (Australian dollar), which I certainly didn't have. I replied whimsically to the email, explaining my situation and very much blaming my circumstances. I was gutted.

A few days later, I got a phone call from an Australian number I didn't know. It was the coach, not his EA. It was Scott Harris, the coach himself. "Hey Simonne, I hear from my team that you've had a bit of a tough run. I don't want to get into it, but I just rang to let you know that I want you to jump on a plane and get to our next event."

I told him, "I know this will help me, but I can't pay."

"Don't worry, I'll waive the fee. Get on a plane, and I'll see you next week," he said, and then hung up.

I couldn't believe it. Someone was giving me a lifeline. Of course, I had no idea how I was going to get to the event in Australia from New Zealand, but I just knew I HAD TO FIND A WAY!

HOW, not WHEN! How can I get to the next step? What becomes possible if I focus on just the next step?

The next day, an accounting client paid their old and small invoice. Just enough to buy a one way ticket. I didn't even tell my partner it was only one way as he drove me to the airport.

I had A$30 in an old wallet that I kept for currency. I had A$17 on an old Opal card. It cost A$15 to get from the airport to my niece and nephew's place, which coincidentally, was on the same street as the venue.

The next day, I walked into the room, and by the end of day one, I knew in every cell of my being that it was the right decision. I wasn't worried about how I would get back home; I just knew I'd made the right decision and everything else would fall into place.

After the first day, I called my partner. It was a Friday afternoon on Elizabeth Street, and I was sitting on the stairs of a corporate office. As soon as my partner answered, I spilt all my excitement to him and shared how much I knew I could do this.

He laughed and said, "I want you to go back tomorrow and sign up for the 12-month coaching."

It was my turn to laugh. "There is no way I can do that! That's more than A$35,000!"

"You're not hearing me. I want you to go in tomorrow and sign up for the 12-month coaching. I believe in you, and I want to invest in you."

I couldn't believe what I was hearing! This is it! THIS is my HOW!

After much negotiation, we made it a business loan.

This was five years ago. I am now 57, one year older than my brother. In the six years since he passed, I have completely changed my life. I have created a seven-figure coaching business, working with accountants and bookkeepers in leadership, who are challenged with burnout, lack of boundaries, and having difficult conversations. I share my journey of near destruction and my tools for how to create and build self-confidence within ourselves. I teach how to eradicate imposter syndrome so we can be who we were always meant to be.

Has it been easy? Absolutely not! In those five years, I've moved towns, and I've lost my mother and my gorgeous sister-in-law. My son was severely assaulted, resulting in the loss of his business and marriage. A botched surgery, leaving him bleeding out in front of us. My partner was in a life-threatening farm accident. We were told he wouldn't survive. Our relationship has had significant challenges with blended families. My business has given me much learning with bad hires and many challenges, and there have certainly been times when I've felt like giving up. And I didn't.

If someone had offered me to rewrite my past, I would have asked, "For what purpose?" If I were to rewrite my past, I would deny myself and others the experience of what it is like to look back with such curiosity and compassion. My past is my privilege; I do not live there. I encourage you to also own all of you and be all of you, the good and the bad.

I can honestly say, hand on my heart, that I am so grateful for the worst times of my life—when I lost my brother, then my contract, and nearly my business. Dropping to the absolute bottom, and having someone offer me that helping hand, made me realise we don't do this journey alone. There are people who see the best in us when we cannot see it ourselves.

When we focus so much on the bigger picture and struggle to make any progress towards it, we deny ourselves the opportunity to be who we are really meant to be. Conversely, when we do the small things we say we are going to do, the next little HOW, it becomes a small victory, a vote if you will, towards the type of person we want to be.

You turn around one day, and you are running a seven-figure business.

You turn around one day, and you and your trainings have won international industry awards and accolades.

You turn around one day, and you're being asked to contribute a chapter to a book.

You turn around one day, and you are who you said you were going to be.

You turn around one day, and realise you've found the pill you were searching for all along.

About the Author
Simonne Liley

Simonne Liley is a founder, trainer, and coach. She has spent years of her life crippled by a lack of self—confidence. This lack spurred a change upon realizing that she was not alone and many of her peers were crippled in the same way. With 25+ years in the accounting industry, she has seen industry legends rise and fall from excessive empathy and burn out. She aspires to change these tragic endings into successful turnarounds.

For the last six years, she has focused all of her passion into coaching and training other directors to help them build their practices their way without sacrificing profit or self. She has coached and trained leaders in heart-centered leadership and trained their teams in conscious communication. She does this by identifying, understanding, and removing disempowering patterns that impede others from reaching their full potential.

If you'd like to know more about her and wish to have an open, non-judgmental conversation, please visit her website or email below.

Contact Information

Website:

www.coreleadershipinstitute.co.nz

Email:

simonne@coreleadershipinstitute.co.nz

Chapter 12

Fearless

Jai Cornell

"And we're broke...AGAIN!" I groaned to myself as I reflected back on my year, wondering how my life turned into what it was.

The year is 2008, at the peak of the worst winter that Washington has seen in almost fifty years. The house that we lived in could barely be considered a house. We had no heating, despite it being below freezing indoors. Even our fridge decided to quit because everything outside of it was colder than inside. Not that it mattered, my family was eating out of cans because the stove also quit working. Only one room had a door, and it wasn't the single bathroom shared among three. We tried to use a portable space heater, but trying to run more than one in the whole house caused the circuits to trip. Our only option was to pile into my daughter's room, the only room with a door, huddling together between a single twin bed and pop-up chair. The only silver lining to look forward to were no bugs. How pathetic! Even bugs didn't want to live with us!

Again, I had no idea how I ended up here.

My entire childhood was spent in poverty. I always had the basics, but never more. I thought I could break the cycle when my children were born. I was determined to break it. I didn't. Sure, I broke other generational cycles like abuse, neglect, substance use, and many more, but I couldn't break the poverty cycle. Each year, I swore I would do better, and every year I fell further and further behind.

My luck didn't change until 2007, when my daughter was in her senior year of high school. I finally got a new position, got a raise, finished school, no longer had my checks garnished, and was in a serious relationship with someone who could provide for himself and didn't need to rely on me. We weren't rich by any means, but we were comfortable and planning for the future.

The future I speak of is that of my daughter, who asked if she could attend the University of Washington. However, since she was underage, she would not be able to live in the dormitories, and I was certainly not letting my underage, overly-sheltered daughter find a roommate off campus. The only choice I had was to go with her. I knew I had to do it, not just for her, but for me too. I needed to escape this island I had always known and expand my horizons. I was working with the same company. I had been with for over ten years, I paid down my debts, I was in a loving relationship, and my life was FINALLY stable! Was this decision the right move?

Going back to the 2008 winter in Washington, I didn't think this was the right move. Not only was our house barely a house, but we were so far from being where I thought we would be. My daughter went to a community college instead of the University of Washington because she didn't qualify for financial aid. My partner, who was promised a job, no longer had one because the position was locked. He had to return to active duty and serve a year in Iraq. We got married out of necessity to ensure we at least had health and dental coverage while he was away. With all the education and experience I had, I thought I would have a somewhat decent job, but instead I was barely getting above the minimum wage and no overtime while working 60-80 hours a week. This was not the life I had thought we'd have at all.

For a moment, I almost regretted not listening to fear when it told me to stay. I should have kept doing what I knew, never changed, and always remained the same. I finally had stability, and like an idiot, I gambled it away for the unknown prospects of the "grass being greener on the other side."

What I didn't know then was how rapidly my life was going to change in just nine months. My husband returned from his tour in Iraq that summer, went back to the reserves, and found a great paying job. With our combined income, we qualified for a loan and started looking at houses. We settled on a company that built homes from the ground up, we could even pick our plot. It only took a week to get everything finalized, and building began. Within the month following, I also started a new position for much better pay and fewer hours.

Life continued on an upward slope from here, but it never would have happened if I never took the chance to leave. If I had stayed in Hawaii because I was too afraid of the unknown, too afraid of failure, then I wouldn't have achieved the success that I have created now.

Fear of failure has been the monster in my closet that has shaped and controlled my every move, every decision, and nearly every thought. My fear was a shadow that made living and experiencing life difficult, if not unbearable. Fear, combined with the vanity to see things the way I saw them, made for a life of unhappiness, a lack of drive; and overachievement created an environment where everything was monotonous. Remaining unchanged seemed like a better fit for my life. Pursuing something new meant possible failure, and the success of anything meant it was only a matter of time until I failed. My life was filled with the fear of everything. It didn't matter what I did, there was always a negative consequence, whether the outcome was good or bad.

It took leaving the safety of what I knew to realize that there comes a time in life when carrying the baggage of these fears becomes unnecessary. I broke that when I moved from Hawaii to

Washington, and that was the start of my transformation! I decided I didn't want to be controlled by fear. I wanted to be fearless, hungry for life, and surrender to God by taking the punches, the ups and downs, and the challenges. I had a complete and utter realization: life owes me nothing, and it could all go away in an instant.

One thing I have learned is that fearlessness is not lack of fear but the strength to talk with the fear and getting up again after falling. Fearlessness is made by not fearing ourselves, by not seeking perfection in our imperfect lives, and by going after whatever it is that we are working toward. It is about facing our fears head on and continuing to move forward despite them.

To anyone standing on the edge of wanting change and feeling fear and scared and not knowing what they want to do with their lives or being constantly reminded of unfinished business, I want to tell you this: the journey of revealing and embracing your demons is full of just that…JOURNEYS!

It takes a true leap of faith, not only in believing what has been decided for you, but it also takes vulnerability, resilience, and failure. The journey of embracing a life fearlessly requires a leap of faith in what has been decided for you, a vulnerability like no other, a resilience like never before, a failure like you've never experienced, and a weakness that you must face head on.

I now understand that the courage to be without fear was nothing. The fears that whispered with a small voice during my silent moments, the insecurities that showed up in my sleep—they were all nothing. Subconsciously, these internal battles were as burdensome as any of my external encounters with my adversaries. However, overcoming these internal battles is the real key to my salvation and transformation.

This journey is a profound lesson in vulnerability. Fearlessness is not only about not fearing failure but also about being open to it and not being afraid of it hindering my journey. It's about being vulnerable. Vulnerability means strength, the willingness to show and expose myself for who I really am, my dreams, and my goals in life. Basically, all my cards are out there, and regardless of the results, it's a freeing status of being out of self and egos and out of any "fitting in" categories to conform to being "successful."

As I reflect on my journey at this moment, I realize that moving to the other side of fear has truly given me a different view of the world. The problems of life and stretches of time are still there, but it doesn't have the same control over me as it did before. Whereas before, I would have seen these challenges or uncertainties of life as doom and gloom. Now, it is a chance for change and growth, a reminder of just how important and precious each moment of our lives are. To live each moment to the fullest with passion and appreciation.

To live with no fear means giving my absolute all, even if that means failing miserably at something. "No fear" means not thinking about failure, fear of rejection, or wanting or having to do something to impress someone else. To not fear the unknown or the different, surround yourself with people who want to help you become better rather than trying to be better to impress someone.

My greatest hope in sharing this story is to inspire others to embark on their own journey of self-discovery and ultimate transformation. To anyone feeling trapped by fear, bogged down by the past, or paralyzed by the future, remember, it's never too late to change your story. And what it takes to live a splendidly fearless life is simple, though often grossly uncomfortable. It is the decision to face your fear, challenge the so-called BS story in your head that's keeping you comfortable and stuck, and grant yourself permission to thrive.

Fearlessness is a choice. That I am certain of.

It is a commitment to live life YOUR way. It is a journey about finding patience, sometimes acceptance, and sometimes never surrendering, but the journey is always wide open.

According to Napoleon Hill, all accomplishments start with a desire as well. A desire isn't an authentic desire if you hope or wish to accomplish it. It must be a desire that's so strong that it takes precedence over everything else in your life.

About the Author
Jai Cornell

Jai Cornell serves as an Executive Director for Maxwell Leadership, offering coaching, speaking, and visionary authorship through the Permission to Flourish anthology series. With a focus on leadership development, Jai has been a source of inspiration for professionals in various industries, notably the aerospace sector. In addition to her professional endeavors, Jai is dedicated to philanthropy and community service, using her expertise to drive positive change and a culture of support and empowerment.

Her work as a visionary author and entrepreneur reflects her commitment to creating accessible pathways for brand growth. Jai encourages others to lead purposeful, passionate lives and pursue flourishing with confidence.

Contact information :

Facebook: https://www.facebook.com/yiayiacornell
Website: www.permissiontoflourish.net
Website: www.jdmwow.com
Email: info@jdmwow.com

EPILOGUE

PERMISSION TO FLOURISH: BREAKING FREE FROM FEAR

By Jai Cornell

Every story written in this anthology is a spark of inspiration. We are reminded that fear can hold us back from making the changes we need to make, keep us from pursuing what we truly desire, or keep us trapped in the present moment while time continues to move. On the other hand, we also see that fear can be countered by courage, determination, willpower, and self-confidence. Fear is only an obstacle, like many other events in our lives.

Within these stories, we have seen the trials that our writers faced, but each and every single one of them chose to confront fear head-on in their own unique way. Anxiety and self-doubt would not keep them bound. They chose to fight back. Through their battle with fear, they developed resilience and growth, leading to endless possibilities and strength that they never knew existed.

In our most trying times with fear, we learn what we are truly capable of. It just comes down to whether or not we will choose to confront fear or let it win. If you should choose the path against fear, you will find yourself walking toward a new experience and new life. When our coauthors broke free from the chains of fear that kept them bound, they pushed forward onto a better path, creating a life of excitement, passion, and hope.

The coauthors have shared their deepest, most profoundly vulnerable moments in the hopes that you will recognize your own strength to conquer your own fears by using various methods and coping mechanisms to do so. Choose the path beyond fear with courage as your guide.

Thank you for choosing to read
Permission to Flourish: Breaking Free From Fear!

Made in the USA
Columbia, SC
07 May 2024